DANCING GAMES
for children
of all ages

By **ESTHER L. NELSON**, M.A. Dance Education

illustrations by **SHIZU MATSUDA**

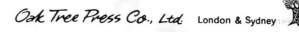

S STERLING PUBLISHING CO., INC. NEW YORK

Oak Tree Press Co., Ltd. London & Sydney

CONTENTS

Before You Begin	3
Postman, Postman	5
Here We Go on Our Ponies	6
Punchinello	7
Who Has a Nose?	8
Susie's Sitting Sewing	10
Jumping, Jumping, Jumping, Jumping	11
Come On Boys and Girls and Hush Your Talkin'	13
One Elephant Went Out to Play	14
The Magic Rope and Limbo	15
There Was an Old Woman and She Had a Little Pig	16
Two Little Blackbirds Sat on a Hill	18
Shoo Fly, Don't Bother Me!	20
Christmas Is Coming	22
As I Was Walking down the Street	24
Jimmy Crack Corn	26
Johnny Works with One Hammer	28
With My Hands I Clap Clap Clap	29
Ach Yah!	30
Over in the Meadow	32
Hokey Pokey	34
Come On Girls (Boys), We're Going to Boston	36
Way Down Yonder in the Pawpaw Patch	38
Comin' Round the Mountain One by One	40
Five Fat Turkeys Are We	42
Mexican (Hat) Clap Dance	44
Square Dance	46
Ya Tsa Tsa, Via La La	50
Bow Bow Bow Belinda (Virginia Reel)	52
Kookaburra	55
Hush Little Baby	56
Sissie in the Barn	58
Korobushka	60
Rain Dance	62
Che Che Koole (African Chant)	64
Hoop Dancing Games	66
Jumping through a Hoop . . . The Sailboat . . .The Eagle Game . . . The Boardwalk	
Ball Games	68
Pass the Ball . . . Roll the Ball	
Jump-Rope Games and Jingles	70
Young Folks, Old Folks . . . Boom Boom, Ain't It Great to be Crazy?	

Fifth Printing, 1974
Copyright © 1973 by Esther L. NELSON
Published by Sterling Publishing Co, Inc.
419 Park Avenue South, New York 10016
Distributed in Canada by Saunders of Toronto, Ltd., Don Mills, Ontario
British edition published by Oak Tree Press Co., Ltd., Nassau, Bahamas
Distributed in Australia and New Zealand by Oak Tree Press Co., Ltd.,
P.O. Box J34, Brickfield Hill, Sydney 2000, N.S.W.
Distributed in the United Kingdom and elsewhere in the British Commonwealth
by Ward Lock Ltd., 116 Baker Street, London W 1
Manufactured in the United States of America
All rights reserved
Library of Congress Catalog Card No.: 73-83456
Sterling ISBN 0-8069-4522-2 Trade   Oak Tree 7061-2469-3
4523-0 Library

Distributed to the music trade by Belwin Mills Publishing Corp.

Acknowledgments

I would like to thank my mother, Freda Nelson, my daughters, Mara and Risa, and my husband, Leon Sokolsky, who gave me the love, courage, and help necessary to get this book together. Thanks to Bruce Haack, my good friend and colleague, for sharing the joys of helping children to express themselves through dance and music. Also thanks to Professor Judy Schwartz of New York University for introducing me to the African Chant, *Che Che Koole*. And to my first and best dance teachers, Katya Delakova and Fred Berk. And sincere thanks to Sheila Barry, an editor whose taste, sensitivity and judgment made it all painless and possible.

BEFORE YOU BEGIN

Learn the dance yourself before you present it, so that you are quite sure of the music and the movements. Explain the form of the dance to your group before you start, so the children know what is expected of them. When you ask them to make a circle, for example, do it with them. Whenever possible, don't tell them what to do—show it to them. That is much more meaningful, and it gives you greater authority. The children feel secure when you are in control and when the demands made on them are clear. If you plan ahead which games you will use, you can work out the transitions between them and keep each session moving along at a good pace.

It is easiest to start off with a game that originates at the piano. These dances are free, require no partners, and no exact positions. For example, "Jumping, Jumping" is an excellent start for a session. From there you can move on to a group circle dance that requires no partners. Then it's a simple matter to go around the circle and pair off the children. Do it fast and they won't have time to object.

Throughout the class—or party—keep the tempo sharp, short, and direct. Never let the rhythm drag. You can use your voice to control the group. Just vary the sound level from loud to soft for effect. A few spots are pointed out where this works especially well, but experiment on your own. Dramatic pauses get the full focus of the group.

It is important for each child to have a turn being in the center for the circle dances. It is even worthwhile jotting down the names of those who had a turn today, so that when you repeat the dance at a later time, you can give turns to different children. If you ask who was in the middle last time, all memory fails, somehow, and though you did the dance many times, nobody remembers having gone inside. Everyone wants to have another turn.

It is difficult to define the dances in terms of age. When a dance is for younger children, it means that you can teach it to three-year-olds, but of course, you must consider your group. There are four-year-olds who are quite sophisticated because they have been exposed to the arts, and there are seven-year-olds who have to move slowly because they lack comprehension. The degree of physical co-ordination which children possess varies greatly. Some six-year-olds can't skip, and it doesn't pay to make an effort to teach them. When their bodies master the co-ordination, it will come, almost as if by itself. If you make a point of teaching it, you only frustrate the child.

Just as literary classics transcend age, so do dances. Start with the first things in this book and work up to the more complex games. Where "for older children" is specified, don't attempt it until your students are at least seven or eight, and then again take their backgrounds into account.

These games are really jumping-off points for discussions of many things, since they run the gamut from elephants to old men, from pawpaws to mother spiders. Every one of them can be a learning experience leading to a discussion of word meanings and relationships. Each new session can be a running dialogue, a constant exchange of response and feeling. The dances are an outline for you to build on. Never let a dance or game start and end with just what is here. If the directions say "Walk," remember that you can also run or jump, hop or fly. Ask the children for their ideas, for interesting variations. Encourage them to think and invent and contribute.

Singing

If you find the children balk at singing along, you are not alone. This has been an era of non-participation, and even young children seem to have lost the knack of joining in. It is immensely important, though, and needs constant encouragement from you. Stop the dance in the middle if the children are not singing and remind them to sing. Some of them really don't know how! Don't be afraid to demand it again and again until they learn. Soon it will become natural and spontaneous, and you won't have to insist on it any more.

When you are about to play songs that you haven't used for a while, ask the group to identify them. Ask them to "open their ears" and listen to the song. If they know what it is, they are not to say a word—just raise their hands and you will call on them. This trains them to listen and develops their musical ear.

For Special Occasions

Many of these games are particularly good to use when you have visitors to your class. Not only can you present them just as they are, but you can invite your guests to join the children. They may object at the beginning, but they will love it and want to do more. Just remember that they don't have the energy of the youngsters and become winded easily. Guest participation is double fun when parents come to visit. Ask the children (whisper to them) to invite their parents to be their partners. This becomes a joyous event for both children and parents. I have known fathers to reschedule their business trips abroad, so they would not have to miss watching their children and dancing with them.

For Special Children

These dances are designed for immediate satisfaction on the part of all children. That holds true for the slow, the mentally retarded and the physically handicapped. As you go through the book, start with the very simplest dance and gradually build up to the more difficult ones. All children have a very good feeling when they learn to do something together, special children too. Make the directions clear and don't be afraid to repeat them.

For Reluctant Joiners

Some children will hold back and refuse to join the group. Don't insist. Just let them sit and watch for a while until you feel that they're anxious to participate. That is the time to offer your hand in a personal invitation. If the child accepts your hand, the problem is solved and the child is unlikely to return to the sidelines, but keep him near you in a circle or as your partner until he feels comfortable in the group. Some children are harder to woo and will take longer to win over, but be patient. Include them in a "name" game, draw them into a discussion, and don't let them see that you care. They will join, because they can't resist.

Accompaniment

The musical arrangements presented in this book are quite simple and adequate. If you can embellish them with ease, do so. If you play the guitar, or an autoharp or zither, fine. You can use the piano as your home base, sing and dance the games through with the children, and return to the piano after you've explained the movements. But if you feel you want to stay right in the dance, do it. You can use records; many of the songs are available in recorded form. You might want to tape the songs in the order you want to use them. If you are lucky enough to have a pianist, this is the most effective system.

Whatever accompaniment you use, and whatever the material, if you've been working with children, you probably know that the spirit of the leader—you—is the most important ingredient. Give the games and dances your own spark and joy of living and change them to suit your classes and yourself. Explore. Experiment. You can't miss.

POSTMAN, POSTMAN

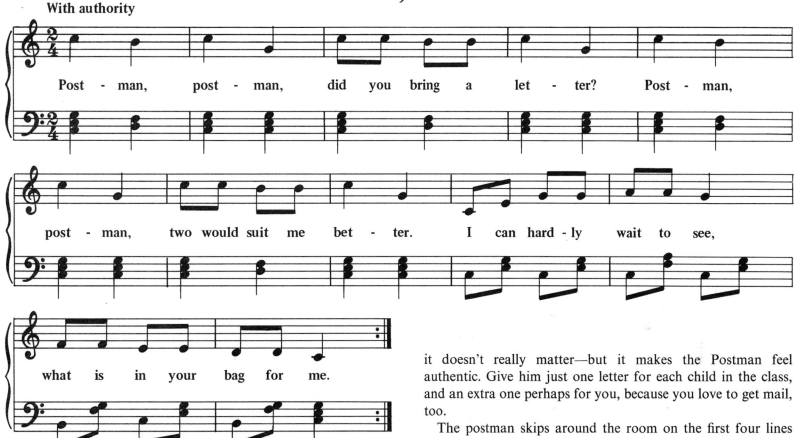

With authority

Post - man, post - man, did you bring a let - ter? Post - man, post - man, two would suit me bet - ter. I can hard - ly wait to see, what is in your bag for me.

This song is especially successful with young children starting at age three. For days before we play this game in class, I save old envelopes so that the postman can have a pocketbook full of mail, and can give each child a letter.

Introduce the game by asking, "What person comes to your house six days a week, even though it rains, shines, storms," etc. They may make a few wrong guesses. Younger children will tell you the answer is their Grandma. But after a bit, they will hit upon the right answer.

Choose one child to be the Postman and give him a large shoulder bag, to approximate the one a real mailman carries. It can be your pocketbook, or a basket, or a shopping bag—

it doesn't really matter—but it makes the Postman feel authentic. Give him just one letter for each child in the class, and an extra one perhaps for you, because you love to get mail, too.

The postman skips around the room on the first four lines of the song, while the children, gathered around the piano, sing. On the last two lines of the song, while the children are still singing, the postman skips back to the group, puts his mailbag down on the floor, and taking out his letters, gives one to each child. (Sometimes it is difficult for the younger child to fish in the bag for the letters, so let him carry them in his hand while he skips around. As long as the mailbag is on his shoulder, he feels official.) Ask younger children, who don't know how to read, who sent them their letters. Allow each child a turn to tell you who the letter came from—Grandma, my cousin, Snoopy, the President, a friend, etc. Older children are apt to give you clever, way-out answers.

Now choose another child to be the Postman, and start the dance again. This time, ask what the letter says.

HERE WE GO ON OUR PONIES

Galloping

Here___ we go on our po - nies, our po - nies, our po - nies, Here___ we go on our

po - nies, Whoa, whoa, whoa.___

Interest in ponies has no age limit, and though this is an easy little dance, done with partners (one of whom is the pony, and the other the rider), all children will enjoy it. It is also a good warm-up for any other activity you want to lead into—they can ride there on a pony.

The child who is the pony extends her arms behind her, and the rider stretches her arms forward and holds the hands of the pony.

There are two basic steps: the first, a gallop around the room for the first three lines. Suggest that they really lift their knees high when they gallop, so they can get way up in the air. Try to make the ponies aware of the pony track, which runs along the outside of the room. Otherwise, they crowd toward the center and the space for galloping becomes smaller and smaller

until they start bumping into each other. On the last line "Whoa, whoa, whoa," the rider steps backwards and pulls the pony back with him on each "whoa." After doing the complete sequence twice, have the pony and rider change places, so that each child will get a turn to be both horse and rider. Make sure the children understand that when they change places, it is with the very same partner, as some of them will start to look for a new one.

When working with young children it is a good idea to explain what the word "whoa" means.

VARIATION: If you have hoops, put the pony inside the hoop, holding onto the front, with the rider outside the hoop holding onto the back with arms spread.

PUNCHINELLO

Oh look who is here, Pun-chi-nel-lo lit-tle fel-low. Look who is here, Pun-chi-

nel-lo lit-tle dear.

1

Oh, look who is here, Punchinello little fellow,
Look who is here, Punchinello little dear.

2

What can you do, Punchinello little fellow?
What can you do, Punchinello little dear?

3

We'll do it too, Punchinello little fellow.
We'll do it too, Punchinello little dear.

This is another easy circle dance, which can include any number of children. It appeals more to the young age group.

One child is chosen to be Punchinello, and he goes into the center of the circle. The other children walk leisurely around the circle and on the word "Look," they point a finger at Punchinello, while continuing to walk around him. This feeling of accent, and its repetition in the second line is very satisfying to the children. They love the strength of their voices in unison and the emphatic movement, which is almost a lunge at Punchinello.

During the second stanza all the children face Punchinello, clap their hands and sing, "What can you do, Punchinello little fellow," etc. He, in turn, does a simple movement for them in place in the center of the circle. If the child has trouble

thinking of something, make a suggestion to him. It can be an awkward situation for a shy child with all eyes on him. He can hop on one foot, for example, or turn, or wave his arm. The children will catch on after the first few times and think of good movements on their own.

As the children sing the last stanza, they imitate the movement of Punchinello, who then picks a successor.

WHO HAS A NOSE?

I am thankful to the French for many things, and one of the most important of them is "Frère Jacques." It is a perfect, short, clear answer song, and there are so many questions!

Gather your class around you at the piano, or at your guitar, or autoharp, or just around you if you plan to sing. You sing the first line, "Who has a nose?" and the children sing back "I have a nose." When you get to the end of the stanza, all clap and sing together, "Now we know, now we know." I find it helpful, especially with the younger children to point to each body part as you sing about it. I have mentioned only a few parts of the body, but don't stop here. This song is an excellent tool for teaching young children just where an elbow is, and a wrist, and an ankle. Enumerate the body parts, each and every one.

The second, third and fourth stanzas investigate just what each body part can do. Again carry on beyond the outline I have given you. "Who can nod your head?" and "Who can wiggle your hips?"

The fifth stanza takes these movements up from the floor to a standing position and the sixth verse takes the movement into space. The possibilities are infinite as you move around the room. Develop your own combinations. Always finish with the words and clap on "Now we know, now we know."

This ending gets the group ready for the next stanza.

VARIATION: You can change the song to talk about animals and how they move. For example: "Who can fly like a hummingbird?" "Who can waddle like a duck?"

For older children you can discuss family relations. "Who has a mommy?" and "Who has a grandpa?" and "Whose Daddy is a teacher?" You can even quiz the children on their school subjects using this song. For example, "Who was the first President?" and "Who invented the telephone?"

Another way of using this song is "Who came to school in a car?" and "Who came on the bus?" This can go into realms of fancy which the children love, such as "Who came to school on a motorcycle?" and "Who came to school on an ocean liner?" and "Who came to school on a plane?" "Now we know, now we know."

If you would like to make the song a bit more personal, call each child by name. "Whose name is Sharon?" and she will sing her answer. "My name is Sharon." "Whose name is Kevin?" etc.

When you have exhausted your own imagination, ask your students to continue the song, and they will carry it on for a long time with many new ideas. Don't forget that you have to fit the words into the music, as each variation has a different amount of syllables and you will need to vary the melodic line to fit your questions.

You can adjust this very valuable song to the needs of your class. It is especially good for shy children, because they can sing in a group. With handicapped youngsters, you can ask of them only things they can perform well. If you are working with young children, you can sing it slowly, while with older children you can zip through at a fast clip. Whatever group you are working with, the song offers immediate rewards: the children know exactly what is expected of them. The structure is clear. Your demands are explicit and easy to fulfil. With the security of knowing what to do, the group gains assurance and ease. Have fun!

WHO HAS A NOSE?

(variations on "Frère Jacques")

Factually

Who has a nose? ____ I have a nose. ____ Who has toes?

I have toes. Who has lots of fin - gers? I have lots of fin - gers.

Now we know, Now we know!

1

Who has a nose?
  Answer: I have a nose.
Who has toes?
  Answer: I have toes.
Who has lots of fingers?
  Answer: I have lots of
  fingers.
Now we know,
Now we know!

2

Who can wiggle your nose?
  Answer: I can wiggle my nose.
Who can wiggle your toes?
  Answer: I can wiggle my toes.
Who can shake your fingers?
  Answer: I can shake my fingers.
Now we know,
Now we know.

3

Who can shake your shoulders? etc.
Who can clap your hands?
Who can scratch your nose with your toes?

4

Who can walk on your elbows?
Who can walk on your nose?
Who can walk on your knees, if you please?

5

Who can stand up very tall?
Who can jump and touch the ceiling?
Who can turn on your tippy tippy toes?

6

Who can walk backwards?
Who can jump and turn?
Who can slide around the room?

9

SUSIE'S SITTING SEWING

Gently and sweetly (lots of pedal)

Su - sie's sit - ting sew - ing, in her lit - tle hous - ie. No one comes to

vis - it her ex - cept a lit - tle mous - ie. Rise, Su - sie, rise,

o - pen your eyes. Turn to the east, and Turn to the

west, and Turn to the ver - y one that you love best.

SUSIE'S SITTING SEWING

This song is especially loved by young children for its magical romantic quality.

"Susie" (sing the name of each child as she goes into the center of the circle for her turn) sits on the floor in the middle of the circle. She makes believe that she has a needle in her hand, and is busy sewing. (If girls or boys object to sewing when it is their turn, substitute another activity such as sawing.) The children in the circle hold hands and tip-toe around Susie, singing the first stanza softly.

They stop before the second stanza starts and face the center of the circle. On the word "Rise," they gesture with their hands to Susie, who slowly stands. On the words "Open your eyes," Susie and the other children make a large movement as if rubbing their eyes, and then extend their arms straight out to the side in a complete stretch. On the words "Turn to the east," the children get up on their toes, with their arms still extended, lift their heads and chests and turn. Then they change direction on "Turn to the west." On the last line "Turn to the very one that you love best," they reverse direction again, and Susie has the difficult task of choosing the friend that she loves best. It may take her a long time. Prod her to come to a quick decision, so that you don't lose the interest of the group, or the momentum these dances carry with them.

VARIATION: Ask one of the children to choose you, the leader, to go into the center of the circle. As the circle moves around you and you sit on the floor and sew, catch in turn every child's eye, and they will laugh with glee. When it comes your turn to choose the one you love best, always choose all of them. Just spread your arms, beckon them in and give them all a hug.

JUMPING, JUMPING, JUMPING, JUMPING

When done with lots of gusto, this song and dance will generate great enthusiasm which will be contagious and you will hate to stop. Of course, since it is up to you (and the children), it can go on indefinitely. The only thing to stop it is fatigue, as it uses up loads of energy, so stop before the exhaustion point.

The dance is just as direct as the words themselves. Since it is so strenuous, it is best for the children to focus on your directions while doing the movements. Don't ask them to sing this one.

Have the children spread out around the room, stand up tall, heads up, chests up, arms down, and looking directly at you. As you sing, they start to jump just where they are, not moving from their spot. When you come to the last line, "Stand-so still," everyone must stop dead and not move—not even breathe. There should be a great pause, full of anticipation. Use it dramatically, stretch it out, look from one child to the other, while everyone's eyes are intently focussed on you for the least clue as to when you will break the silence. After the next stanza comes the same loaded pause. Vary it from stanza to stanza. Make some of the pauses short, make some of them almost nonexistent, and make others so long that the children are almost at the point of frustration, but go on before their patience runs out.

This song is especially successful with slow children. You can put into it the things they already can do, such as walking or jumping. Hopping is a difficult co-ordination for many of these children, so explain to them that they must hold one foot up in the air, and jump on the other. It may take them some time to master, but patience and repetition bring results. Again, be sure to explain that this is hard for many children to do, and it takes time to learn.

VARIATIONS: Ask older children for their suggestions, for more difficult co-ordinations, such as leaping, run-run-skipping, skipping and turning, etc. They will invent many more, and hard ones too, since they do love the challenge of inventing new movements and doing them.

JUMPING, JUMPING, JUMPING, JUMPING

Very perky and jumpy

Jump-ing, jump-ing, jump-ing, jump-ing, see me jump-ing up so high.

No-bo-dy knows I can jump so high. No-bod-y knows I can stand

so still . . .

You can write your own continuation of this song. Some possibilities are:

Hopping on one foot.
Turning on your toes.
Spinning (on the floor) like a top.
Rolling (on the floor).

Rowing a boat to the teacher to finish the song gets your children right back to you.

1
Jumping, jumping, jumping, jumping,
See me jumping up so high.
Nobody knows I can jump so high.
Nobody knows I can stand-so-still. . . .

2
Jumping and turning, jumping and turning,
Round and round and round I go.
Nobody knows I can jump and turn.
Nobody knows I can stand-so-still. . . .

3
Walking backwards, walking backwards,
Walking backwards, here I go.
Walking backwards carefully,
Nobody knows I can stand-so-still. . . .

COME ON BOYS AND GIRLS AND HUSH YOUR TALKIN'

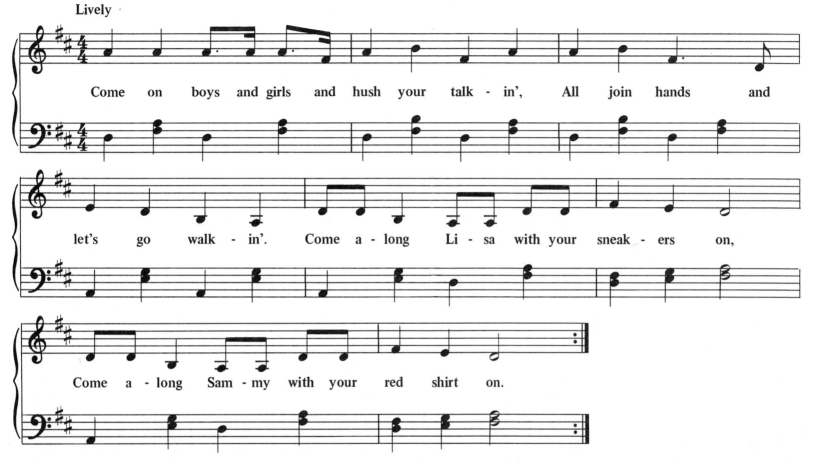

Lively

Come on boys and girls and hush your talk - in', All join hands and

let's go walk - in'. Come a - long Li - sa with your sneak - ers on,

Come a - long Sam - my with your red shirt on.

This is one of the favorite songs of all children, because it singles them out and besides calling them by name (which all children love), it offers something special and descriptive about them. It has infinite possibilities, as all good songs do.

For the first stanza, walk around the room (you might choose a mature child to do this, while you play the piano), as everyone sings the first two lines. As you walk, move in various shapes around the room, instead of the usual circle. Weave in and out, around, and back and forth. When the last two lines of the first stanza are sung, and a particular child called, that child gets up and joins hands with you. As the song progresses, each child called joins hands with the child

before, so a long line forms behind you. When all the children are in line, skip around the room with the line and lead the group into a circle. They are now ready for another dance that calls for a circle formation.

If you want to do a short version and end it quickly, just say,
Come along the girls that have blue eyes on,
Come along the boys that are wearing pants, or

Come along the children that have two ears on.
It will take them a while to catch on, but they do—sometimes one at a time—and in comes the rest of the group.

ONE ELEPHANT WENT OUT TO PLAY

Dignified

One el - e - phant went out to play down by a

sand - y beach one day. He had ___ such e -

nor - mous fun that he asked an - oth - er el - e - phant to come.

ONE ELEPHANT WENT OUT TO PLAY

Line dances are especially useful since they work with any number of students. If you have a small class, call each child separately to join your line. If your class is large, call several children at the same time. Be flexible and adjust each dance to the needs of your class.

Start this line dance by asking the children to clap only on the underlined words, as you play and sing for them. Also ask them what the word "enormous" means. (This is a good way to teach vocabulary and synonyms. You can use other words like colossal, stupendous, tremendous, etc.) After they know when to clap, have them stand in place and instead of clapping, have them jump on those words. When they know this, you are ready to start.

If you are not free to lead the dance, choose one of your responsible students to be the Mother or Father Elephant.

On the first and second line the leader (Father or Mother Elephant) walks around the room, then stops and jumps in place on "beach one day." This pattern repeats with the third and fourth lines, jumping on "phant to come." The leader looks out at the group of baby elephants and says "Come ooooooooon, Jane." Jane gets up behind the leader and puts her hands on the leader's waist. Now the leader starts to count the baby elephants, puts a hand on his or her own head and counts "one," then on the head of Jane and counts "two." I always ask the children to bend their knees when the leader's hand is on their head, and then to straighten right up. When the counting is over, the song starts again, but this time we sing, "Two Elephants went out to play, etc."

This song continues until all the elephants have been chosen to come along. If your class is large, choose two or three or four elephants at a time. The children find it exciting if you make it more dramatic by counting the elephants "ah-*one*," "ah-*twoooo*," "ah-*threeee*," etc. When all the elephants are on line (as the last one, always choose the teacher who is playing the piano—the children love it), finish with these words, "But there weren't any other elephants to come!"

THE MAGIC ROPE AND LIMBO

A rope is even better when it's magical. You can make your rope special by tying scarves together, one color after another (be sure to tie them loosely so you can get them apart). Even if you use a plain jump rope, or a piece of clothesline, though, the rope is magic, because the children are going to fly over it.

Choose a child to hold the rope with you, and have the children form a line, facing the rope. Then each one gets up on her toes and, one by one, lifts head and chest and runs to the rope, leaping over it. Start with the rope almost on the floor. When each child has had a turn and lines up, waiting to return on the other side of the rope, lift the rope a little bit. Some children are very timid and need a great deal of encouragement to attempt the leap. They stop when they get to the rope and shake their heads sadly. Lower the rope for such a child, so he doesn't get frustrated and totally discouraged.

Continue the game until the rope has gone as high as you think the children can leap. Then hold it as high as you can and ask, "Do you think you can jump over this?" There will be an outcry of "No," with an occasional "Yes," from a brave soul. Then you say "All right, I'll let you run underneath the rope, but make sure you don't touch it." Of course, you continue to lower the rope each time, until the children have to crawl under it. This is called LIMBO and is lots of fun. As the rope lowers, tell the children they can get further down by leading the movement with their hips, and bringing the top part of their bodies behind them.

VARIATION: When you do this with older children, let them do a current dance step while going under the rope.

THERE WAS AN OLD WOMAN AND SHE HAD A LITTLE PIG

Perky

There___ was an old wom-an and she had a lit-tle pig___ oink, oink,

oink. There was an old wom-an and she had a lit-tle pig. It___

did-n't cost much and it was-n't ver-y big.___ Oink, oink, oink.

This song is intended for younger children, certainly three-year-olds can do it, but you will be amazed at how much the older ones enjoy it. The preschoolers will want it over and over again, but if you use it with older students just once in a while, it will be a big success.

I always start this song with a discussion of language, how we communicate and how animals do it. When we come to the "oink, oink, oink" part of the song, the children nod their heads up and down three times, one for each "oink," since this is the way pigs talk. Once they understand this, they will even nod later on when they are all curled up and the "oink" part repeats.

The dance starts with the children sitting at the piano, while the teacher either plays the piano and sings, or just sings. The children nod their heads at the "oinks." The words are self-explanatory. During the second stanza the pigs curl up, close their eyes and go to sleep. They sleep through stanza three. Before the fourth stanza starts, choose one child to be a farmer, or if your group is large, choose a few children to be farmers. The farmers tip-toe around and tap the pigs gently on the top of the head. As each pig feels the tap, it lifts its head and wakes up. In stanza five, both pigs and farmers roll on the floor out to the end of the room. On stanza six, they all roll back to the teacher, curl up and go to sleep again.

THERE WAS AN OLD WOMAN AND SHE HAD A LITTLE PIG

1

There was an old woman and she had a little pig, oink, oink, oink.
There was an old woman and she had a little pig.
It didn't cost much and it wasn't very big.
Oink, oink, oink.

2

Those little pigs curled up in a heap, oink, oink, oink.
Those little pigs curled up in a heap.
They shut their eyes and they went to sleep.
Oink, oink, oink.

3

They slept and they slept and they slept and they slept, oink, oink, oink.
They slept and they slept and they slept and they slept.
And they slept and they slept and they slept and they slept.
Oink, oink, oink.

4

The farmers woke them up one by one, oink, oink, oink.
The farmers woke them up one by one,
And then they rolled out in the sun.
Oink, oink, oink.

5

They rolled and they rolled and they rolled and they rolled,
    oink, oink, oink.
They rolled and they rolled and they rolled and they rolled.
And they rolled and they rolled and they rolled and they rolled.
Oink, oink, oink.

6

Those little pigs rolled back to their pen, oink, oink, oink.
Those little pigs rolled back to their pen.
And then they went to sleep again.
Oink, oink, oink.

TWO LITTLE BLACKBIRDS SAT ON A HILL

Sweetly

Two lit - tle black - birds sat on a hill. One was named Jack and the

oth - er Jill. Fly a - way Jack, la la la la.

Fly a - way Jill, la la la la. Come back Jack,

la la la. Come back Jill, la la la la la.

TWO LITTLE BLACKBIRDS SAT ON A HILL

This dance is done with two groups of children. The size of the group does not matter, and it is no problem to include any number you happen to be working with. It is especially useful for young children, because it gives them a chance to change rôles and teaches them to listen carefully to words and music, so they move at exactly the right time.

Divide the children into two groups, and put each group in a corner of the room (corners near). One group becomes the "Jack" birds, and the other the "Jill" birds. I usually go to each group, and pointing to each child in that group, I say "I'll bet you thought your name was Sally or Debbie or Rita. Well it's not, now your name is Jill." Make very clear to the children who they are: it is not so easy for the young child to assume an identity other than his own. Then explain that when you say "Fly away, Jack," all the Jack birds will spread their wings, get up on their toes, and fly directly across the room to the diagonally opposite corner. This is repeated with the Jill birds.

Then each group is invited to fly back to its original corner. The difficult part for the children is to wait for each group to have a turn before they fly back. You will have to explain this carefully to them. When the song has been sung and danced through once, I say to the children "Now, change places," and of course not only do they change places, they also change names. So go over it once again, from the beginning, and make sure that each child knows now who he is, what his name is, and which corners he is to fly to.

SHOO FLY, DON'T BOTHER ME!

With enthusiasm

Shoo fly, don't both - er me. Shoo fly, don't both - er me.

Shoo fly, don't both - er me, For I be - long to some - bo - dy. I

feel — I feel — I feel like a morn - ing star, I

feel — I feel — I feel like a morn - ing star.

SHOO FLY, DON'T BOTHER ME!

This is a simple circle dance with couples, easy-to-learn, fun to sing, and young children can do it easily. Sing it with lots of gusto and always accent the word "Shoo."

The partners take hands and form one big circle. Still holding hands, everyone skips four times to the circle center on the first line, and then out again, skipping four times on the next line. Repeat this for the next two lines.

On the second stanza everyone drops hands, and the couples give each other both hands, and skip around each other until the end of the second line. Then they remain in the circle, but they have changed places, so that each one is where the partner was when the stanza began.

As the dance starts again, each dancer takes a new partner, the dancer on the other side. The dance repeats and partners always end the second stanza in the same way, so that this dance can continue until you meet your own partner (if the group is not too big, this is possible).

Since this dance uses the skipping step throughout, and skipping is tiring, the dancers may be exhausted by the time the dance is over. If the circle is too large for them to get back to their original partners, stop the game in the middle. Never dance to the point of exhaustion; it's not worth it. Children love to use their energy and need this physical release, but it is possible to overdo it.

VARIATIONS: As the dancers skip into the center of the circle in the first part of the dance, suggest that they lift their hands, so when they reach the circle center, all hands are lifted high, and as they go back from the center they lower their hands.

Try doing it on tip-toe, and talking or whispering or singing softly.

Try marching and singing loudly.

The more variety the better. Even try doing it backwards, for a change. Hold hands facing the outside of the circle, and move toward the center.

When you're working with older age groups, do the dance first in the standard way. Then when you repeat it, after the first stanza, on the "I feel" section, ask one child to be the leader and do a movement in place, which everyone will copy. The child is free to do the "twist" or "monkey," etc. Then everyone repeats the dance from the beginning. On the next stanza choose a new child to pick a movement that all can follow.

CHRISTMAS IS COMING

This old English song makes a delightful dance, and one that the children will ask to do over and over, as each one of them will surely want a turn to be the "old man." I found an old black bowler hat in my closet, and bring it out every Christmas for just this purpose. The next thing to do is collect lots of pennies, about three for each child. If you can get new shiny pennies, it's even better, and you are all set to start.

One child, who is picked to be the old man, puts on his hat. Each of the children (sitting on the floor in a group) is given one penny, and the old man starts to skip around the room while everyone sings. Explain that the old man would skip in a heavy way, since he cannot move as easily as a young child. The old man skips for the first two lines of the song. Then he comes back to the group of children, carefully takes off his hat, and walks over to each child, who gently puts his penny into the hat, for the remaining lines of the song.

Be sure to explain that the old man will come to each child separately; otherwise they all descend upon him with their pennies at the same time, reaching over each other. The old man, in a dignified way, bows to each child as the penny drops into the hat. When the old man has collected all the pennies, he shakes them in his hat, so we can all hear them jingle.

When a new child is chosen to be the old man, this time give him two pennies for each child. Young children especially, love to get money to put into the hat, and will immediately ask if they can keep it. Just explain that you need it for other classes. This dance can go on until you feel that the children have had enough; just promise to finish it another day, so that all children can have a turn. I think three times is enough, as you always want to end on a "high" note, when there is still enthusiasm left, rather than when the class is sated.

CHRISTMAS IS COMING

With dignity and seriousness

Christ-mas is com-ing, The geese are get-ting fat. Please to put a pen-ny in an

old man's___ hat. Please to put a pen-ny in an old man's hat. If you

have-n't got a pen-ny, A ha' pen-ny will do, And if you have-n't got a ha' pen-ny, Then

God bless___you!

AS I WAS WALKING DOWN THE STREET

With lots of spunk and gaiety

As I was walk - ing down the street, hi - ho, hi - ho, hi - ho, hi - ho, A

lit - tle bird - ie I chanced to meet, Hi - ho, hi - ho,___ hi - ho.___ A

rig - get - y jig and a - way we go, Hi - ho, hi - ho, hi - ho, hi - ho, A

rig - get - y jig and a - way we go, Hi - ho, hi - ho___ hi - ho.

AS I WAS WALKING DOWN THE STREET

1

As I was walking down the street,
Hi ho, hi ho, hi ho, hi ho,
A little birdie I chanced to meet,
Hi ho, hi ho, hi ho.

2 (Chorus)

A riggety jig and away we go,
Hi ho, hi ho, hi ho, hi ho,
A riggety jig and away we go,
Hi ho, hi ho, hi ho.

3

As I was walking down the street,
Hi ho, hi ho, hi ho, hi ho,
A little froggie I chanced to meet,
Hi ho, hi ho, hi ho.

Chorus

4

As I was walking down the street,
Hi ho, hi ho, hi ho, hi ho,
A puppy dog I chanced to meet,
Hi ho, hi ho, hi ho.

Chorus

5

As I was walking down the street,
Hi ho, hi ho, hi ho, hi ho,
A big long snake I chanced to meet,
Hi ho, hi ho, hi ho.

Chorus

6

As I was walking down the street,
Hi ho, hi ho, hi ho, hi ho,
A kangaroo I chanced to meet,
Hi ho, hi ho, hi ho.

Chorus

7

As I was walking down the street,
Hi ho, hi ho, hi ho, hi ho,
My teacher, Miss Nelson, I chanced to meet,
Hi ho, hi ho, hi ho.

This is one of those wonderful songs that can go on and on to extend to many areas of a child's life. For the first stanza, each child walks by herself around the outside of the room. Explain that there is no need to walk in a circle: it is a nice feeling to be free. Since a bird is mentioned during the second stanza, the children get up on their toes, lift their heads and chests, and run, moving their arms up and down alongside them. Make sure they bend their wings at the elbow a bit, so the arms are not very stiff. Also explain that the feeling of a bird is "up" and light, and if they plod heavily they will not be able to stay up in the air.

As you move to the third stanza and a new animal, change the means of moving down the street, so now it becomes walking on your heels, or jumping down the street, or running. The children all know how to be frogs, or puppies. Here you can add, "Stand still and wag your tail. Remember that puppies never walk on their knees. They walk up on their feet—on four legs. Now can you chase your tail around—faster and faster and still faster? Did you catch it?"

When you come to the big long snake, don't forget to explain that a snake has no hands, so they will have to put their hands behind their backs and use their hips and shoulders to push themselves along the floor. Tell them to wiggle and wriggle and jiggle. That's quite a bit of fun, and not so easy.

The kangaroo bends his wrists, and holds them up in front of him. When he jumps, he bends his knees and brings them up in front. "Can you jump backwards, Kangaroo?"

When I say "My teacher, Miss Nelson, I chanced to meet" I also add, "Come and say hello and sit down near the piano." This ends the dance and your class is back with you, ready to sing or go on to another activity.

I use the first word of the song "As" as my attention-getter, and tell the children that whenever they hear that word they have to stop wherever they are and just stand motionless. "Don't move, don't even breathe." This gets them into the palm of your hand, as they are totally focussed on you, and you can proceed to the next stanza. Vary the "As"—stretch it out, trill it, make a song out of it, sing an arpeggio with it. Use it to hold the children, and make it dramatic. It always works.

JIMMY CRACK CORN

Seriously (with tongue in cheek)

When I was young I used to wait On Mas - ter, and give him his plate, And

pass the bot - tle when he got dry and brush a - way the blue tail fly.

Peppy

Jim - my crack corn, and I don't care, Jim - my crack corn, and I don't care,

Jim - my crack corn, and I don't care, My Mas - ter's gone a - way.

JIMMY CRACK CORN

1

When I was young I used to wait
On Master, and give him his plate,
And pass the bottle when he got dry,
And brush away the blue tail fly.

Chorus

Jimmy crack corn, and I don't care,
Jimmy crack corn, and I don't care,
Jimmy crack corn, and I don't care,
My Master's gone away.

2

And when he'd ride in the afternoon,
I'd follow after with a hickory broom,
The pony, being rather shy,
When bitten by (by what?) the blue tail fly.

Chorus

3

One day he ride around the farm,
The flies so numerous they did swarm,
One chanced to bite him on the thigh,
The devil take (take what?) the blue tail fly.

Chorus

4

The pony run, he jump, he pitch,
He throw my Master in the ditch.
He died and the jury wondered why.
The verdict was (was what?) the blue tail fly.

Chorus

5

They lay him under a simmon tree,
His epitaph is there to see.
Beneath this stone I'm forced to lie,
A victim of (of what?) the blue tail fly.

Chorus

This is one of America's favorite songs, a spirited gutsy song, so play it that way on the piano. It can be sung just as a song, or you can add movement to it, as I do during the chorus, to make it even more lively.

Sing each stanza, sitting around the piano. Have the children pantomime words such as "give him his plate" and "pass the bottle" (take a drink from a water bottle) in the first stanza, and when you come to the first chorus have them clap.

The second stanza is just sung, except that when you come to the words "when bitten by," stop the music and ask "bitten by what?" and the children will answer with the music.

On the next chorus, ask the children to continue with the clapping but this time to stand, look at you, and jump as they clap. You will see only beaming faces, for children cannot jump or skip without smiling. When the chorus is over, they must sit down near the piano right away, so you can continue without losing momentum.

On stanza number 3, sing until you get to the word "bite," when the children reach forward with their heads, open their mouths wide and bite into space. It is also a good thing to ask them where their thigh is, as young children may not have any idea of its whereabouts. After the start of the last line, "The devil take," again ask, "Take what?" and the answer will be "The blue tail fly."

On the next chorus, make it more difficult. This time instead of jumping and clapping, add a turn, so now they are clapping, jumping, and turning on one spot. Remember to have the children return rapidly to place at the end of the chorus.

The fourth stanza is sung as above, with the usual question and answer. On the next chorus, I have the children spread out around the room, leaving space between, get up on their toes, stretch their arms out to the side, and then turn as fast as they can. If they go too fast, have them change direction in the middle —that should help unwind them.

The last stanza is sung in the same way. On the last chorus, I tell the children they can make whatever movement they want: it usually turns out to be a jumping one.

JOHNNY WORKS WITH ONE HAMMER

Strong and accented

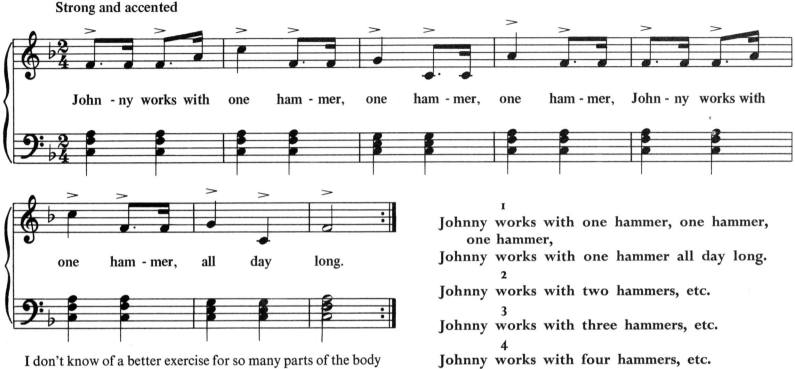

John - ny works with one ham - mer, one ham - mer, one ham - mer, John - ny works with

one ham - mer, all day long.

1
Johnny works with one hammer, one hammer,
  one hammer,
Johnny works with one hammer all day long.

2
Johnny works with two hammers, etc.

3
Johnny works with three hammers, etc.

4
Johnny works with four hammers, etc.

5
Johnny works with five hammers, etc.

I don't know of a better exercise for so many parts of the body than this song. Do it in a circle, sitting near the piano, spread out across the room, or in whatever form you find works best.

I usually introduce this game with a discussion of houses, buildings, and what materials you need to build them: "Windows and door," the young children will say. "Electrical sockets and water pipes," say older ones. Finally we get down to the very basic hammer, and we are ready to start.

The children sit on the floor with legs stretched out in front of them and feet touching. The first hammer is the arm, with fist clenched, moving directly up and down perfectly straight without bending the elbow. (If you bend the elbow, you don't have enough strength to knock the nails in.) The second hammer is the other arm, so that both arms work in the second stanza. The third hammer is one leg. As each "hammer" is added, the rest continue to work. The fifth hammer is the head which also moves rhythmically up and down. When you come to the fifth hammer, tell the children to lean back a bit before they start (this makes it easier to lift their legs), and with five hammers they have both arms, legs and head all moving at once. This is quite a strenuous dance, and so after the five hammers, Johnny is tired, and draws his knees up to his chest, puts his head down on his knees and goes to sleep.

VARIATIONS: With older children, to make it technically more demanding, ask them to point their toes when they lift their legs, and then next time do it with a flexed foot. Or make it harder, by keeping the feet apart, and the arms apart, so the movement takes on a different shape. Also change the name "Johnny" to the names of the children in your class. Or change the child's name in each stanza.

WITH MY HANDS I CLAP CLAP CLAP

Light and playful

With my hands— I clap clap clap. With my foot— I

tap tap tap. One two three, One two three. Round a-

bout so mer - ri - ly.

This simple group dance is performed in a circle without partners and learned in one easy try. Use it with any group, young, old, slow or special.

Before you start this song, as you stand in a circle, say "Get your hands ready to clap, but don't do it until I tell you to." With the words "clap clap clap" on the first line, everyone claps. Then with one foot extended they tap with their toes on "tap tap tap." On the third line all join hands and slide to the left (with heads and chests high). On the fourth line all drop hands, stretch them to the sky, get up on their toes, and turn in place.

After the first stanza everyone faces the circle center, puts hands on hips and waits for the words "thump thump thump,"

1
With my hands I clap clap clap.
With my foot I tap tap tap.
One two three, one two three,
Round about so merrily.

2
With my hips, I thump thump thump.
With my feet I jump jump jump.
One two three, one two three,
Round about so merrily.

3
With my fingers I snap snap snap.
With my palms I slap slap slap, etc.

when they shake their hips from side to side. With hands still on their hips, for the second line, they jump in place three times.

The last two lines repeat the movements of the first stanza.

Make sure the children join you in singing the song. The words are easy to remember and sing and add a great deal to the dance.

ACH YAH!

ACH YAH!

This is a charming German couple dance, good for all ages. It is especially useful when you have a mixed age group. Have each young child choose an older child as his partner. The young children feel honored to be dancing with an older child, and the older one feels protective towards his partner. It is an excellent dance to use when parents come to visit, too. They love doing it with their children as partners.

Explain that the words "Ach yah" mean "Oh yes" in German. This is danced by very proud peasants who are marching to the fair, so partners link elbows and march in a circle formation with their knees up high for the first two lines of each stanza. On the words "Ach yah" the couple drop hands, face each other, and bow. The girls curtsy by putting one leg behind the other and bending their knees, arms out to the side. The gentlemen put one hand across their middle front, one hand across their middle back, and bend from the waist. On the second "Ach yah," they turn back to back and bow again.

On the third stanza the partners hold one hand, skip around the room for all the tra la la's, and stop in time for final "Ach yah" bows. Change partners and start the dance again.

VARIATIONS: With older children, have them do the first part of the dance backwards. Make sure they lift their knees high as they walk, even though they are going backwards. For the third stanza, return to the original pattern and skip forward.

Another variation is to have the older children, instead of holding hands and walking forward, walk alone in a diamond shape. At the first "Ach yah," each child will be out in the first line of the diamond. The partners still face each other and bow, even though they are some distance from each other. On the second stanza they walk again, but this time in the second line of the diamond, which brings them back to their partners, in time to bow on the 'Ach yah." The skipping is done as usual.

OVER IN THE MEADOW

Softly, with magic

O-ver in the mead-ow in a nest in a tree, Lived an old Moth-er bird-ie and her lit-tle bird-ies three. "Fly," said the Moth-er, "We fly," said the three, So they flew and were glad __ in the nest in the tree.

1

Over in the meadow, in a nest in a tree,
Lived an old Mother birdie, and her little birdies three.
"Fly," said the Mother. "We fly," said the three,
So they flew and were glad in the nest in the tree.

2

Over in the meadow, in the sand in the sun,
Lived an old Daddy froggie and his little froggies one.
"Hop," said the Daddy. "We hop," said the one,
So they hopped and were glad in the sand in the sun.

3

Over in the meadow, in a sly little den,
Lived an old Mother spider, and her little spiders ten.
"Spin," said the Mother. "We spin," said the ten,
So they spun and were glad in their sly little den.

4

Over in the meadow, in a house behind a door,
Lived an old Mommy pussy cat,
            and her little kittens four.
"Creep," said the Mommy.
            "We creep," said the four,
So they crept and were glad
            in their house behind the door.

5

Over in the meadow, in the deep blue sea,
Lived an old Mother, Father, Grandpa, Grandma, etc.
            fish, and her little fishes three.
"Swim," said Everybody. "We swim," said the three,
So they swam and were glad in the deep blue sea.

OVER IN THE MEADOW

This dance is one of my favorites, and judging from the faces of the children, as they do it, one of theirs, too.

The child who is the Mother or Father initiates the movement during line three of each stanza, and then on line four the children imitate that movement. Use as many or few children as you have in your group. Numbers are no barrier. Feel free to have the children make up new stanzas. Don't feel you have to stick with the already existing ones. Help the children with ideas, and they will come up with brand new verses.

Choose a child to be the Mother bird. She stands on her toes in front of the group of little birds sitting bunched together in their nest, and lifts her wings in the air. On the words "Fly, said the Mother," she flies around the room, moving her wings up and down and taking small running steps with her feet. Tell her to bend her wings a bit at the elbow, and really get them way up and way down as she goes. On the words "We fly," the baby birds come out of their nest, and fly on their toes in the same way, behind their Mother, once around the room and right back to their nests.

A new child is chosen to be the Daddy frog. Girls can be daddies as well. On "Hop, said the Daddy," the Daddy frog jumps as high as he can, and lands on the floor, with both hands on the floor between his bent legs. The baby frogs follow on the words "We hop" and they all hop around the room on both feet, right back to where they live. It is a good idea to have the Mommy or Daddy animal start out in their proper movement position. The Daddy frog, for example, should be out in front of the group with hands on the floor between his legs, feet spread apart, knees bent, and bottom almost touching the floor.

A Mommy and Daddy spider spin by moving their fingers, bending their elbows, and moving one arm over the other near the middle of the chest, while turning on their toes, and stretching their bodies up high. Tell the children not to look at the floor, because that way they'll get dizzy. Remind them to lift up tall and keep stretching up, with their heads high.

With the pussy cats, remind the children that cats do not walk on their knees, but on four legs, up on their feet, with their tails high. For some children this is difficult and will take a bit of time. Be sure to explain that they must lean on their hands and put weight on them, so the four legs move evenly.

In the last stanza, if you have a large group, and many of the children have not yet had a turn to be either a Mother or a Father, now is the time to get them all in by calling for a grandmother, grandfather, aunt, uncle, cousin and teacher fishes. Give out all these rôles, and if there are not too many baby fish left to follow it is all right. The children with special rôles lie on the floor and wait for the words "Swim, said Everybody." As in the other stanzas, when you say "We swim," the remaining fishes swim out into the deep blue sea. Since swimming is a movement that doesn't cover too much space and is tiring, after the stanza is finished, tell the fish to turn around and swim back to where they came from. If possible, when playing this stanza on the piano, put it into a waltz form. The waltz rhythm is very good for swimming!

If at the end of each stanza, the children are not yet through with their movements and are not back in the places they started from (always use a corner as their "home" or "nest"), repeat the last two lines of music, without words. That should be enough to get them back in place, ready to start the next **stanza.**

HOKEY POKEY

Jazzy and lowdown

You put your right hand in, You put your right hand out, You put your right hand in, And you shake it all a-bout. You do the ho-key po-key And you turn your-self a-round. That's what it's all a-bout. HEY!

HOKEY POKEY

1

You put your right hand in,
You put your right hand out,
You put your right hand in,
And you shake it all about.
    Chorus
You do the hokey pokey
And you turn yourself around.
That's what it's all about.
Hey!

2

You put your left hand in, etc.
    Chorus
3
You put your right foot in, etc.
    Chorus
4
You put your left foot in, etc.
    Chorus
5
You put your big head in, etc.
    Chorus
6
You put your backside in, etc.
    Chorus
7
You put your whole self in, etc.
    Chorus

This dance has no age limitation and, happily, it includes male, female, and neuter genders. Boys will love it, as well as Grandmas, though they may not be able to bend too low.

I have seen this circle dance done in a straight-laced way, but I think it's done better with a jazzy flavor, with a bit of southern drawl, lots of syncopation, and a lowdown, mean, husky voice.

After forming a circle, have the children take one giant step backwards. That will enlarge the circle and put plenty of space between them. On the first line, each child puts his right hand into the circle, at shoulder height. On the second line, he extends the same hand behind him, to the right. On the third line he again puts it into the circle, and then shakes it from the wrist for all it's worth.

On the chorus, each child lifts one index finger up in the air after the other (like the old trucking step) a few inches in front of his ears. Then he turns around in place with small steps, but in a sharp, crooked way, so that he really moves his hips, shoulders and everything else that can move "crooked." Suggest that the child take each step on his toe, and then turn his foot, so his whole body twists. When everyone has completed his turn and is facing the circle center, he bends his knees, gets into a crouching position, with body erect and with hands on knees, and says "That's what it's all about," very quietly, almost in a whisper. Then have them look at you as you give the cue to jump up high, clap their hands, and shout "Hey!"

The dance continues, with the left hand, the right foot (just extend it straight out, and point the toe), left foot, "big" head, and backside (each turns halfway around, so that his bottom is facing the circle center, and bends from the waist facing the outside of the circle, so that his bottom reaches toward the circle center). Between each of these stanzas, repeat the chorus. When you come to stanza number 7, they jump into the circle center, out of the circle center, straight back in again, and then shake all over.

When the children crouch down (on the last chorus), tell them that they have to stay there forever, and can never come up. Tell them they must stay there forever and a day, at least. Later you may (being the good soul that you are) have a change of heart, and decide to let them come up, but hold them there for a while. They will all be focussed on you. When you let them up, do it in a dramatic way. Use the moment, then take a gasp of air (an in-breath) and say your "Hey!"

COME ON GIRLS (BOYS), WE'RE GOING TO BOSTON

COME ON GIRLS (BOYS), WE'RE GOING TO BOSTON

1

Come on girls (boys), we're going to Boston.
Come on girls, we're going to Boston.
Come on girls, we're going to Boston,
Earl-eye in the morning!

Don't we look pretty (handsome)
        when we're dancing?
Don't we look pretty when we're dancing?
Don't we look pretty when we're dancing,
Earl-eye in the morning!

2

Come on boys (girls), we're going to Denver, etc.

Don't we look handsome (or strong)
        when we're dancing? etc.

This is a spirited travelling song which can be danced to by any size and age group. You will have no problem getting boys to pack to go to Boston or fly to Florida and the places you may visit are unlimited. Slow children will find great pleasure in getting ready for a trip and taking off.

Suggest the children open imaginary suitcases and put their sweaters, pajamas, and hairbrushes, etc. inside. The children will have many suggestions. When the suitcases are all packed, lock them up, pick them up and away you go.

On the first three lines, the children skip around the room in a circle carrying their suitcases. On "Earl-eye in the morning," they put down their suitcases, and dance as beautifully as they can, all around the room. Since they have been skipping in a circle, they tend to continue in that form. Explain that they no longer have to keep to a circle, but should dance wherever they want.

If the children are self-conscious about dancing by themselves in an unstructured form, it helps to tell them to use every part of their bodies to dance with. Ask them to move with you as you mention all the parts of the body: the fingers, the wrists, the elbows, the shoulders, the toes, the ankles, the knees, the hips, the chest, the back, the head, etc. Also it helps to ask the children to close their eyes when they dance: when they have no frame of reference and are not aware of anybody watching them, they can focus on themselves and their bodies and the delicious feeling of movement.

Now "open your eyes, and pick up your suitcase where you left it, and let's hop to Hoboken." The dance repeats.

VARIATION: Ask the children to choose another city or country each time the dance is repeated, and another way of getting there. You can run to Rumania, slide to Sweden, turn to Tanzania or jump to Jamaica. It is a good way to teach geography and the difference between cities, states, and countries. One day try it with continents. The children are always full of good ideas, so get their contributions. They are an endless source of new material and new twists for old standbys.

WAY DOWN YONDER IN THE PAWPAW PATCH

Spirited with intrigue

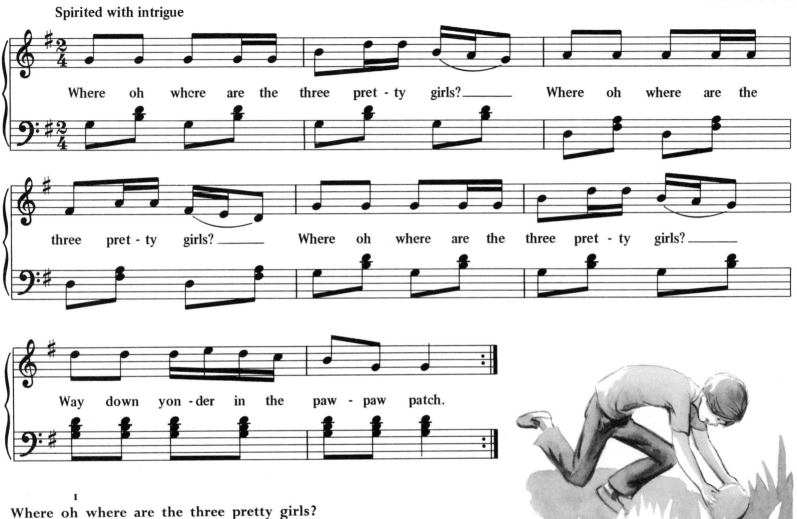

Where oh where are the three pret-ty girls?_____ Where oh where are the

three pret-ty girls?_____ Where oh where are the three pret-ty girls?_____

Way down yon-der in the paw-paw patch.

1

Where oh where are the three pretty girls?
Where oh where are the three pretty girls?
Where oh where are the three pretty girls?
Way down yonder in the pawpaw patch.

2

Come on everybody, let's go find them,
Come on everybody, let's go find them,
Come on everybody, let's go find them,
Way down yonder in the pawpaw patch.

3

Pick 'em up pawpaws, put 'em in your pocket,
Pick 'em up pawpaws, put 'em in your pocket,
Pick 'em up pawpaws, put 'em in your pocket,
Way down yonder in the pawpaw patch.

38

WAY DOWN YONDER IN THE PAWPAW PATCH

Although this song has been in many books, and is quite a common one, try the dance described here, which is not the standard one that you probably know, but my own version.

The first question that the children ask, is "What is a pawpaw?" Tell them it is a large, long yellow tropical fruit like a pa-pa-ya, and that is good to eat, so there is good reason to pick it up and put it in your pocket.

You can use this as an individual dance, with each child moving by herself at her own rhythm. Choose a few girls to start, and as they skip around the outside of the room (with the rest of the class sitting at the piano) they sing, "Where oh where are the three pretty girls?" etc. At the last line of the first stanza, the dancers stop (one foot will be in front of the other), lean way back, and hold up one thumb. They lean this thumb back to one side, and move it in three sharp accented movements toward their backs on the words, "Way down yonder." On the words "pawpaw patch," they bend their knees and, moving the thumb once more behind them, they follow it all the way around so that they have made a full turn.

As the children sing the start of the second stanza, "Come on everybody, etc.," they all make a "come on" movement with one arm and start to skip after the three original pretty girls (who continue skipping around the room). When the words "Way down yonder," in the fourth line reappear, they lift their thumbs and everyone repeats the pawpaw movement, ending with the turn.

In the third stanza, as they are skipping, everyone bends down, but keeps moving, and picks up the imaginary pawpaws and puts them in her pocket, as the song says. With the last line, all repeat the thumb movement with the turn.

Choose new children to start the dance again, five handsome boys, perhaps, and sing "Where oh where are the five handsome boys?" etc. You can use large groups here, and everyone can have a turn and be happy. If your group is small, do it

individually. Choose one child to skip around and sing, "Where oh where is pretty little Laura?"

One trick that helps the dance to work, is to stop the music after the first three lines, and say "Get your thumb ready." It can be a difficult transition, if there is no time in between. After the children learn the dance, perhaps you can do without it.

Special fun on a rare occasion is to have the teacher skip around, and the children sing "Where oh where is Miss Nelson (substitute own name)?"

COMIN' ROUND THE MOUNTAIN ONE BY ONE

Joyously

Oh we're com-in' round the moun-tain one by one, Oh we're

com-in' round the moun-tain one by one, Oh we're com-in' round the moun-tain

one by one, Rise oh sug-ar oh rise. _____

1

Oh—we're—comin' round the mountain one by one,
Oh we're comin' round the mountain one by one,
Oh we're comin' round the mountain one by one,
Rise oh sugar oh rise.

2

Won't—you—show us a little something one by one?
Won't you show us a little something one by one?
Won't you show us a little something one by one?
Rise oh sugar oh rise.

3

That's—a—very pretty something one by one,
That's a very pretty something one by one,
That's a very pretty something one by one,
Rise oh sugar oh rise.

40

COMIN' ROUND THE MOUNTAIN ONE BY ONE

This fun circle dance knows no bounds of age or gender. Boys especially love it.

The dashes after the first two words of the first line of each stanza indicate a pause after each of these words. This device gets everyone's attention and total focus, so you are all ready to start together. After you do the dance a few times, the children will pick it up and sing it that way ever after. It is as if a speaker says "Ahem" before he starts his speech. These two pauses are like the "introduction" to the dance, and they work, especially if you speak sharply, with total silence between each word. When the song hits, it hits with impact, and off you go.

Choose a child to stand in the middle, and make a circle around her. When you go through the dance for the first time, just walk around the mountain for the first three lines. The child in the middle remains still. On the fourth line, drop hands, and have everyone face the circle center. Ask them to take a step backwards to stretch and even out the circle. (As the circle goes around it tends to close in toward the center and become smaller.)

In stanza 2 the child in the center does a movement for us, while the children in the circle sing and clap their hands on the underlined words. If the child in the center has difficulty thinking of what movement to do, help out. Suggest that she jump. If jumping has been done already, and she jumps again, tell her to add a turn, so she will be jumping and turning. As the dance repeats, the children will get bolder and try new things.

In the third stanza, everyone does exactly what the child in the middle is doing, and sings, "That's a very pretty something." Point out to them that they must imitate the movement completely, down to each detail. Explain to the child in the center that she must continue with the same movement so the other children can copy her.

At this point the center child picks someone to replace her inside the circle. She joins the outside circle and the dance starts again.

VARIATIONS: Come around the mountain each time in a different way. You can tip-toe round the mountain, hop, slide, gallop, march, or sneak, and sing, "Oh—we're—sneaking round the mountain," etc.

For older children, a different way to end the dance on the last chorus is to have everyone move closer to the circle center, so that the circle becomes quite small. The children link hands or pinkies, bend way down like ducks, and waddle around the mountain. This is special fun and usually ends in total disaster, with lots of laughter.

FIVE FAT TURKEYS ARE WE

This provides the most fun a dance ever can, as evidenced by the fact that the children ask for it over and over again, even though Thanksgiving has long since come and gone.

First, ask the children to explain what the song is about, as the young ones may not understand that the cook is hunting for turkeys to cook for dinner, and the turkeys are hiding in the tree. Of course, though the cook looks and looks, she can't find them anywhere, and that is why they are still here; otherwise they would be browning in the oven.

Now you have to discuss turkeys. Tell your group that turkeys look like big chickens and move with bodies that are heavy and clumsy. What about their wings? They don't fly like little birds way up in the trees, but how do they fly? Then encourage the children to find their own movements, to feel and move like big, fat, juicy turkeys.

As you sing the first line, the turkeys walk around the room slowly, then stop and shake their heads up and down twice during the pause that follows the words "are we."

During the second line the children continue with their turkey walk. At the word "tree," they stop and shake their heads up and down, so that their red wottles shake, too. Now allow a long pause while the turkeys fly up into the "tree" (designate one specific corner of the room as the tree). In their haste to reach safety, they will forget who they are and fly like little light birds, so remind them they must move like big, heavy, clumsy birds that fly close to the ground.

The first time you play this game, I suggest that you—the adult—be the cook. Just walk around looking for those turkeys as you sing the third and fourth lines, behind the door, on the ground, everywhere. Ask any person not participating if they have seen the turkeys, to which, of course, they will shake their heads and say, "No, I haven't seen the turkeys."

By the end of the fourth line, wander right up to the tree.

Make sure that you never look up at the turkeys—you can't see them, they are covered by leaves. Then turn, with your back to the turkeys, and whisper to them, "Now sneak up behind me, and don't forget to walk like a turkey." Walk toward the center of the room slowly singing line five, and the first word of line six, wait and keep walking slowly. Then suddenly, sharply, dramatically (and with a mean grimace) turn quickly around to face the turkeys. They will automatically scream and run back to hide in their tree. You can run slowly after them, but make sure that they all get back safely. Then you can say "Oh dear, what will I do now for Thanksgiving dinner?"

If some of the youngest children are really scared, and don't want to play the next time, let them join you in being the cook. Most of the children will adore the element of danger, knowing that you will not catch them and that they are safe. Older children can tell more clearly what is fantasy and what is reality, and they will not be afraid. In fact, for a change, you can catch one, and perhaps even put him in the oven. Older children can also do the rôle of "cook" successfully, so give them a chance from time to time, while you play the piano.

Change the time span between the two words of the last line, so they don't know what to expect. Make it a short wait one time, and stretch it out the next. I think repeating this game twice is enough, so that interest doesn't wane, and the children will want it later again and again.

FIVE FAT TURKEYS ARE WE

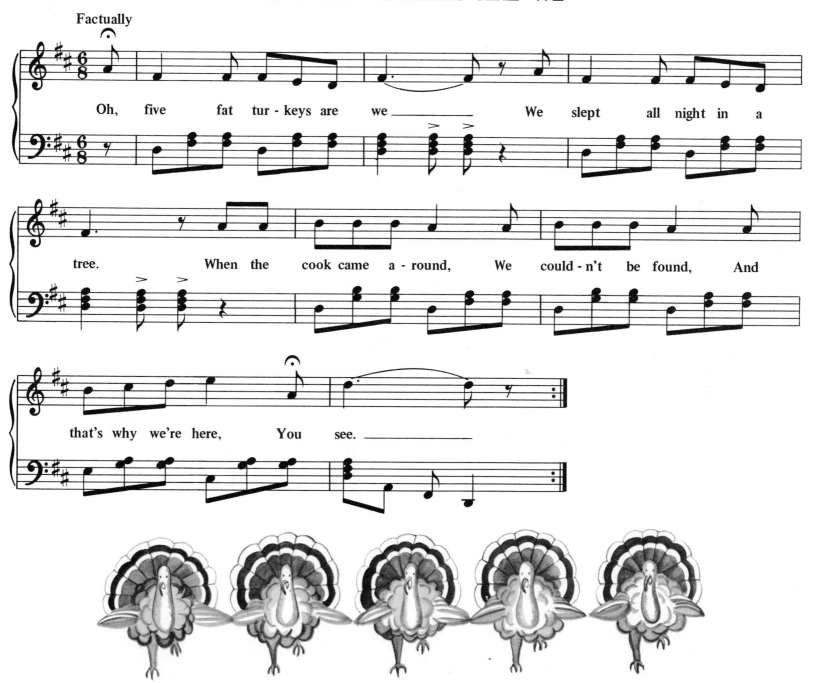

Oh, five fat tur-keys are we _____ We slept all night in a tree. When the cook came a-round, We could-n't be found, And that's why we're here, You see. _____

MEXICAN CLAP DANCE (LA RASPE)

This dance, performed in a circle without partners, is simple and easy for a young group, a slow group, or a group of parents and children, where you want to teach a quick, effective, yet easy-to-learn dance. Satisfaction is almost immediate, and the spirited music makes it an instant success.

You may have tried the dance already in one form or another. In this version, start out simply, having the children give three claps and stop on the fourth beat. Repeat this until you have finished playing the music. By that time the group should have the feel of the rhythm. Then go on to working the rhythm through their feet. Have the children form a circle, face its center, put their hands on their hips, and jump on both feet for the three beats, resting on the fourth.

When they are able to do this, and even young children can do it if you introduce it slowly, have them clap two short quick claps on the fourth beat (directly after the three jumps). This sequence—three jumps and two claps—is performed four times. Then put one hand on your hip, one hand up in the air, get on your toes, lift your head, and turn around and around on your toes until the next to the last measure, when you get down on one knee, lift the left arm way up in the air, and on the last note, shout out "Hey!"

VARIATION: For older children: have partners form a large circle, then drop their hands, and face each other with their hands on their hips, still in circle formation. This time, instead of three jumps in place, they extend the heel of one foot out in front, bending both knees a little bit. Now they jump in the air, and change feet, so that now the other foot is extended with the heel in the front. Jump and make this exchange of feet three times; then give the same two claps. This step of "change and change and change" is performed four times. Then both partners hook right arms (elbow to elbow), hold their left arms up in the air, and skip around each other until the last

measure. Then they stop, lift that left arm even higher in the air, and say "Hey!"

Try doing the dance the simple way the first time, without partners, and the more complicated way the next time, with partners. It keeps the children on their toes, gives them a good deal to think about and remember, and they love the challenge.

MEXICAN CLAP DANCE (LA RASPE)

With Latin rhythm

1   &   2   &   3 Clap, clap etc.

Go a-

round and   a - round and   a - round, etc.

Get down on one knee and say   hey   hey!

SQUARE DANCE

Folksy and fast

One of the best dances ever, the square dance is not limited in the number of children or adults who can participate—in fact, the more the merrier. If you feel confident that the children can choose partners themselves, then let them. Otherwise, just have them form a circle and pair them off yourself. The dancer on the left-hand side is the male, and the one on the right the female.

1

Honor your partner

Boys bow by placing one hand across the middle front, and the other hand across the middle back.

Girls put one foot behind the other, bend their knees, extend their arms, as if they are holding wide hoop skirts and bow. This is the first call, "Honor your partner." The partners face each other (still standing in the circle) and bow.

2

Honor your corner

On the second call, "Honor your corner," each partner turns to the person on the other side and bows again in the same way.

3

All join hands and circle to the left

On the third call, the circle moves together in a walk or a skip. There is no set timing to this dance. Once you give a direction (call), the dancers do that step until you give them another direction. Don't drag out the calls too long. It is better to be quick, and it's more effective, too.

4
The other way back
And make your feet go clickety clack

After the group circles to the left, give the fourth call. They reverse direction and walk or skip to the right, but this time encourage the group to make lots of noise with their feet.

5
Into the center with a great big holler
**Do it again and I'll give you a dollar (maybe, but
  then again on second thought, I won't)**

On the fifth call the circle stops and, still holding hands, everyone walks toward the circle center, lifts their arms, gives a loud shout of "Yahoo!" then walks back again, lowering them. With "Do it again and I'll give you a dollar," this repeats. Always call the directions just before you want them to happen. The last call, for example, is made as the group is coming out of the circle for the first time.

6
All jump up and never come down
Swing your partner round and round
**Till your old wooden leg makes a hole in the
  ground**

In stanza 6, holding hands in a circle formation, everyone

jumps up in the air a few times. Then each couple gives the other both hands and skips around the other, not moving from their basic area.

7
Gentleman sweep the floor.
Lady sweep the floor like you never did before.

In figure 7 the boy gets down on one knee and lifts his right hand in the air. The girl gently holds that hand (a finger is even easier) and skips around the boy. Tell the children to hold arms or fingers loosely, so they can circle without pulling each other down. Then reverse rôles, and girls go down on one knee while boys skip around.

SQUARE DANCE (CONTINUED)

8

Wind up the ball of yarn.
Follow the person in front of you and circle to the left
Never drop hands and keep following that person in front

The last figure is the ball of yarn. Many children don't even know what a ball of yarn is, so ask them about it before you start. Most of them have either seen their mothers knitting, or kittens playing with a ball of wool, if only in books. The ball of yarn starts with a circle to the left, and it is a good idea for you to lead it. It is a tricky figure, and if it gets mixed up, there is no way to straighten it out. As you start to circle to the left, point out to the children that each one must follow the child in front and they must never drop hands. Then you release the hand of the person to your left and wind the line behind you toward the center of the circle.

9

We're going to wind up that ball of yarn
We're going to make it tight and tighter
And when it's very tight
We're going to unwind
And hope it comes out right.

While the circle turns and winds, repeat the words of stanza 9. When you say "We're going to unwind and hope it comes out right," you stop, and follow your left shoulder, reverse your steps, and unwind. Each child still follows the child in front, *and does not change direction.* Leading with your left shoulder until the circle is unwound, then turn and follow your right shoulder, so that the circle rights itself and you can form the original circle and join hands.

10

Honor your partner
Honor your corner
Honor the pianist
Honor the teacher
Take your partner to a nice soft chair
You know where and I don't care.

Stanza 10 explains itself, and that's the end of the dance.

SQUARE DANCE VARIATIONS

VARIATIONS: If the children are older and able to do more complex figures, try these.

Wring out the Dishrag

> **Wring out the dishrag**
> **Keep it wringing till it's dry**

Both partners face each other, give each other both hands, and turn under first one arm and then the other, continuing the turn in the same direction until they are back where they started from. Be sure to explain that the turn continues until it is complete.

California Fruit Basket

> **Ladies, join your tender, lovin' hands**

Starting with a circle, girls directly walk to the center and join hands.

> **Gents, join your black and tans**

The boys make a circle on the outside to this call, slide once around the circle to the left, and stop at the left-hand side of their ladies.

> **Ladies, lift your hands**
> **Gents, get under**

Tell the girls never to drop their hands, *no matter what happens*. The boys bend down, stoop under the girls' arms, and come up inside the circle.

> **Ladies, put your arms down behind your gents**
> **(don't let go)**
> **Get up on your toes, lean back,**
> **And swing to the left like thunder**

On this call, ladies and gents get up on their toes and take small running steps to the left.

> **Now go the other way, you're going wrong**

They reverse their direction.

These steps, "Wring Out the Dishrag" and "California Fruit Basket," will fit anywhere in the dance. The order is up to the caller. Go to it and have fun!

YA TSA TSA, VIA LA LA

This is a charming Israeli couple dance, and it is especially useful when you are working with a group of mixed ages. It begins with a circle as one child walks counter-clockwise in the center, and the circle walks clockwise around her. As they walk slowly and leisurely, everyone sings "la la" until the end of the first stanza.

Before the second stanza starts, the center child selects someone in the outside circle as her partner and goes to face him. She beckons to him with her index finger and skips backwards to the center of the circle, on the first line of the second stanza, with the partner skipping toward her. On the second line, the partner beckons to her with his finger, and skips back to his place in the circle as the child in the center follows him to his place. On the third line, they clap hands once, give each other both hands and skip around each other, with arms outstretched, until the end of the stanza.

At the end, both partners go into the center, the outside circle joins hands, and the dance starts from the beginning, except that now two children are walking counter-clockwise inside the circle. As you can see, the number of children inside the circle increases geometrically (a good illustration of this mathematical principle) until there are half as many children

on the inside as on the outside. At this point, have the inside circle remain still, as the outer circle moves; otherwise, there will be chaos. Also ask the inner circle to move close to each other, so the outer circle won't break.

Of course, the last time the dance is done, everyone will be in the center, and no one in the outside circle. Then you can either finish the dance or start from the beginning.

This is an ideal dance to use when parents visit your group. Do it once with only one child in the center, to show the parents how it works. The second time, ask all the children to go into the center, while the parents remain on the outside. Each child chooses his own parent to be his partner and they all love it.

This dance can be done with all ages, but is best for older children, as it involves many different movements and quick changes of direction. If you want to try it with younger students, do it slowly, and describe every figure before it begins, since they may not be able to remember the order of the movements. You can add a touch of spice by having the person who follows the beckoning finger put her hands behind her back and dance her skipping steps a bit shyly, as if she is not so sure that she wants to come.

YA TSA TSA, VIA LA LA

Playfully

La la la la la la la, La la, la la la, La la la la la la la, La la la la la Eh, ya tsa tsa vi-a la la,___ Ya tsa tsa vi-a la la___ Clap and skip a-round and a-round And a-round and a-round and a-round and a-round. Eh, ya tsa tsa vi-a la, la,___ Ya tsa tsa vi-a la la.___ Clap and skip a-round and a-round And a-round and a-round and a-round and a-round.

BOW BOW BOW BELINDA (Virginia Reel)

With enthusiasm and clarity

Bow bow bow Be-lin-da, Bow bow bow Be-lin-da, Bow bow

bow Be-lin-da, Won't you be my dar-lin'!

The Virginia Reel is an early American dance, and its popularity today proves that it is not only a great dance, but one of the all-time favorites.

It starts with couples forming a line. Try to get space between each set of partners so they will have room to dance. Have the partners drop hands and face each other. Now ask them to take four steps backward, away from their partners. Even out the new lines and start the dance.

1

Bow bow bow Belinda,
Bow bow bow Belinda,
Bow bow bow Belinda,
Won't you be my darlin'?

On the first stanza couples take three skips toward each other and bow, and then four skips back to place. Explain that the bow is a short one, and that they must not linger in it, but go right back to their places. This is repeated during the last two lines of the first stanza.

2

Right hand round, around Belinda,
Right hand round, around Belinda,
Right hand round, around Belinda,
Won't you be my darlin'?

In this stanza, children skip towards each other, take right hands, skip once around each other and then skip back to their places. If there is a problem figuring out which is the right hand (and there often is), ask the children which hand they shake hands or salute with. Usually they know, and you can remind them that it is their right hand. Instead of holding hands, they can also link elbows, go once around quickly and right back to place. Emphasize this at the very beginning, since otherwise children tend to go round and round and won't get back to their lines on time for the next stanza. If they have extra time when they get back before the next stanza, they can stand in place and clap.

BOW BOW BOW BELINDA (Virginia Reel)

3
Left hand round, around Belinda, (3)
Won't you be my darlin'?

The action in the third stanza is the same, except that they use the left hand.

4
Both hands round, around Belinda, (3)
Won't you be my darlin'?

In the fourth stanza, the children give each other both hands, skip around once and go back to place.

5
Do-si-do around Belinda, (3)
Won't you be my darlin'?

For the do-si-do figure in the fifth stanza, the children cross their arms in front of them at shoulder level, skip out to meet each other and then skip around each other, passing right shoulders, without turning, and then skipping backwards to their places.

6
The head couple slide Belinda,
Slide up and down Belinda,
Head couple slide Belinda,
Won't you be my darlin'?

In stanza 6, the head couple (at the front of the line) walk towards each other and give each other both hands. They slide all the way up the space between the two lines, and then slide directly back, while the other children clap. The head couple, when they return to their places (instead of facing each other, as they did throughout the dance), face the front of the room. The other children turn and face the same way directly behind them, so we now have two lines facing front.

7
The head couple lead your line
Around to the back Belinda
Now make an arch Belinda
And everybody skip through.

Each of these leaders now turns to the outside, away from the other leader, and as each line follows its leader, the leaders walk to the back of the line, meet their partners, and together form an arch with their arms. The children on the line meet their own partners behind the arch, take hands, and skip through it, going toward the front of the room. The line reassembles, each couple having moved up one place, and the first leader couple are now at the end of the line. The dance starts again from the beginning.

VARIATIONS: If your group is older and accustomed to more complex steps, try doing the authentic "reel" step in stanza 6. This way, the head couple skip to meet each other, link right elbows, skip once and a half around, and then, with their free left arm, link elbows with the first person on the opposite line. After they skip once around, they link elbows with their original partner and repeat this figure with the next person on the line, until they work their way to the end of the line. The head couple, by that time, arrives at the other end of the line, and they take hands and slide back to place, where stanza 7 is danced as in the simpler version.

In another variation, only the head and foot couples dance, while everyone else claps. The boy at one end and the girl who is on the diagonally opposite end skip to the center towards each other and back on the first half of the first stanza, while the other diagonally opposite couple skip to the second half of the first stanza. This diagonal pattern continues in each stanza through the end of the fifth. The sixth and seventh stanzas are danced as in the simple version. Only use this method with older children, since they have the patience to stand in place, clap, sing, and wait for their turns. The simple version has everyone dancing almost all the time, which makes it easier for young children, who need to be kept moving.

BOW BOW BOW BELINDA

Fun Version—Virginia Reel

Here is my version of this dance, a funny one, especially good for parties and festive occasions. Each call is performed only once. On "Won't you be my darlin'," children return to their lines.

1

Meet your partner, pull her nose, (3)
Won't you be my darlin'?

2

Meet your partner, step on her toes, (3)
Won't you be my darlin'?

3

Meet your partner, pull her hair, (3)
Won't you be my darlin'?

4

Meet your partner and rub bellies, (3)
Won't you be my darlin'?

5

Meet your partner and bump bottoms backwards, (3)
Won't you be my darlin'?

6

Meet your partner, give her a hug, (3)
Won't you be my darlin'?

7

Meet your partner, give her a kiss, (3)
Won't you be my darlin'?

8

The head couple slide Belinda, etc.

This dance makes for a rollicking good time, and is a good one to end the party or session with, as everyone is laughing and happy, and not much can follow it. Don't feel limited by the suggestions here. Make up your own, or ask the children for ideas. For example:

Meet your partner and tickle her chin

Meet your dog and pat his head

Meet your partner and rub her knees

Meet your partner and pull her ear

KOOKABURRA

Kook-a bur-ra sits in the old gum tree,____ Mer-ry mer-ry king of the bush is he,____ Laugh kook-a-bur-ra, Laugh kook-a-bur-ra, Gay your life must be.

Kookaburra sits in the old gum tree,
Merry merry king of the bush is he,
Laugh, kookaburra,
Laugh, kookaburra,
Gay your life must be.

Words and music from "The Ditty Bag," © 1946 by Janet E. Tobitt. Used by permission.

The kookaburra is an Australian bird, a large kingfisher, which makes a loud raucous laughing sound. This dance is for older children, as the timing is precise, with quite a few steps to remember which follow quickly one after the other.

Make a circle. On the first line, take one jump to the circle center, then one jump out, and repeat both jumps. On "Merry, merry," both arms reach up; on "king," both arms come down. On "bush is he," turn in a circle around yourself with small walking steps. On the first "Laugh, kookaburra," shake your shoulders in a pantomime of a laugh. On the second "Laugh, kookaburra," tap the floor in front with your toe.

On the last line, put your hands on your hips; on the word "life," lift your head, and on "be," jump and turn in place for four counts.

Then repeat the dance, but this time jump way into the circle so that your knees are bent and you almost reach the floor. Bring your arms forward in a circular motion as you jump in, starting and ending thigh high. Reverse that arm motion as you jump out.

If you want to get the group back to the piano—or to any special part of the room—use the last four jumps to carry them there. Just give them notice beforehand.

HUSH LITTLE BABY

This is a delicate old American lullaby, and an easy piece to present for any occasion or program. Use a doll as a prop to make it more realistic.

It is a good idea to start with a discussion of what a lullaby is, and how many other lullabies the children know. Then choose one child to be the mother. She makes believe she has a baby in her arms.

I
Hush little baby, don't say a word
Momma's gonna buy you a mocking bird

For the first stanza, she gets on her toes, and turns and dances softly while she rocks her baby. Then tell her to put her baby down carefully and sit with the group.

HUSH LITTLE BABY

2
And if that mocking bird don't sing
Momma's gonna buy you a diamond ring
Choose another child to be the mocking bird, who then spreads her wings and flies around the room during stanza 2.

3
And if that diamond ring turns brass
Momma's gonna buy you a looking glass
Before you start the third stanza, ask the children what a diamond ring is, and what is special about it (besides the price). Finally they will tell you that it sparkles and shimmers and shines, so the child you pick to be the diamond ring must stand in one spot and shake and shimmer all over. Encourage her to use every body part.

4
And if that looking glass gets broke
Momma's gonna buy you a billy goat
The child who is the looking glass in the fourth stanza should walk on stiff, straight legs, on her toes, with her arms stretched up, a bit rounded to look like the shape of a mirror, and with fingers touching. On the words "get broke," she should fall down and stretch out as if scattered into a thousand pieces.

5
And if that billy goat won't pull
Momma's gonna buy you a cart and bull
The billy goat in stanza 5 must bend down low, put his hands on the side of his head like horns, and buck with them as he runs, leaning forward, and kicks his legs way up behind him.

6
And if that cart and bull turn over
Momma's gonna buy you a dog named Rover
Stanza 6 can be done with two children; one, the bull, puts his hands behind his back, and the other holds onto his hands as the cart. They walk with slow, heavy steps, lifting their legs in the air, until the words "turn over," when they drop hands and fall down on the ground and roll and roll.

7
And if that dog named Rover won't bark
Momma's gonna buy you a horse and cart
The dog named Rover in the seventh stanza walks on four legs until the word "bark," when he looks to you for his cue. When you are ready, nod your head once, and Rover barks once. Make this quite clear.

8
And if that horse and cart fall down
You'll still be the prettiest baby in town
Stanza 8 is done with two children, who assume the same positions as in stanza 6, but this time they both gallop until they "fall down."

9
So hush little baby don't you cry
'Cause Daddy loves you and so do I.
Now the original mother emerges once more, with her baby in her arms, rocking it and dancing and turning on her toes for the first line of stanza 9. On the second line, she gets down on one knee, still rocking her baby, looking at it, and finally bending down and kissing it.

When the children know their rôles and their movements, repeat the dance, but this time let each child take all the parts. If it is too complicated to work in pairs, as in stanzas 6 and 8, do them singly, so you don't lose the continuity of the dance. At the end of the dance, so that the spell is not broken by children dropping their babies on the floor, tell them to put the babies into their cribs at the side of the room, and tuck them in for the night.

SISSIE IN THE BARN

Sissie in the barn,
The barn O'Leary,
Sweetest little gal
I ever did see.

Oh barn barn,
Put your arms around me.
Tell me little Sissie,
What you think of me.

"Stay back gal,
Don't cha <u>dare</u> come <u>near</u> me,
After <u>all</u> those <u>sassy</u>
<u>Things</u> you <u>say</u>."

Oh barn barn,
Put your arms around me.
Tell me little Sissie,
Will you marry me?

I learned this dance when I was 12 years old in a summer camp, and I have never come across it since. Girls love it, because it gives them a chance to dance close to the boys. It is distinctly a couple dance, and definitely for older children as there is an element of flirtation involved.

Have the partners form two long straight double lines, girls on one side and boys on the other. All face their partners. Make sure beforehand that there is space between each set of partners, as they will have to turn around each other and that takes room.

Partners hold hands, and each takes a step to the same side, the boy starting on his right foot, and the girl on her left. Now tap the other foot near the one that took the step. Repeat the same movement to the other side. Let the arms sway along from side to side with the feet.

This step is done for the first stanza as everyone sings along. The couple can also lean from side to side as they do this step.

On the second stanza, the couple move into an old-fashioned dance position, close to each other, and do the same step from side to side. They can use it to turn in position, leaning from side to side as they turn, moving their arms up and down with each side step.

On the third stanza, the girl (apparently having whispered in the boy's ear what she thought of him, which wasn't very flattering) cowers back from her partner, to take her punishment. She turns half away from him, bending her knees and putting her hand over her mouth, as if she is ashamed of what she said. She stays in this position, as the boy stretches his arm directly out at the girl, points his finger angrily at her and says,

> "*Stay* back *gal*, don't cha *dare* come *near* me
> After *all* those *sas*sy *things* you *say*."

On each stressed word, he points his finger accusingly at her and almost shouts out the word. This is rhythmic and should have a beat, and a hillbilly accent, if possible.

On the last stanza, the boy and girl move into a close dance position and turn around each other just where they are, with the same side step.

At the end of the final stanza, all say "Shift" in a loud voice, and the line of girls moves up one, while the first girl goes to the end of the line. Each person now has a new partner and the dance can begin again. It should be danced with lots of hillbilly spunk, and don't be afraid to exaggerate the flirting and coy elements which make it such special fun.

SISSIE IN THE BARN

KOROBUSHKA

KOROBUSHKA

This authentic Russian dance is for older children, and the steps are more complex than those in the previous dances. Children of 8 may be able to do it (7, if they are adept at dance and bright).

Start with a line of partners with space between each couple. Teach the first step in place. It is 3 steps and a hop, which means that each time you do it, it starts on a different foot. When the children have mastered it individually, have them give their partners both hands and do the step together. The boy starts backwards on his left foot, while the girl starts forward on her right foot. The first step is repeated three times, changing direction each time.

When the children do the step together easily, add arm movements to it. Still holding hands, one set of arms extends straight out and moves forward, as the other set moves back. The forward arm is always up straight; the back arm is always bent. The arms go back and forth with each step, 3 times, and they are held in the last position as the children hop. This repeats 3 times as the feet repeat.

On the last line of the first stanza, the children jump, first with feet crossed, then with feet apart, then with feet together. Practice this step individually—the children love to do it—and practice it continually, since the dance must be done quickly, and the sequence must be smooth.

The second stanza starts with a 3-step turn. The partners drop hands and each one takes 3 steps to the right (away from each other), each step a half turn. On the fourth count, they rest. Then each partner returns with the same 3-step turn going to the left. The turn to the right starts with the right foot and follows the right shoulder around, and the reverse is true when you turn to the left.

On the third line of the second stanza, partners give each other right hands and take one step on the right foot toward each other, tapping with the left foot behind the right and raising their arms. Then they step back on the left foot, tapping with the right. On the last line of the second stanza, they change places by walking three steps forward.

In stanza 3, repeat the 3-step turn to the right and then to the left for the first two lines, from the new positions. On the last lines, the partners change places again and are back where they started, ready to repeat the dance.

VARIATION: To add to the style of the dance, after each 3-step turn, instead of resting on the fourth count, have the children clap and hop on the right foot in the right-step turn, and on the left foot in the left-step turn.

After the children have mastered the steps, teach them the words, so they can sing as they dance. Singing makes it even harder, as there is so much to think of at one time. When your group knows the dance well, ask their parents to join them in it when they come to visit. The parents will have trouble with the dance, but they will be doubly impressed by their children's ability.

RAIN DANCE

62

RAIN DANCE

This dance was performed by American Indians as a prayer for rain. Do it with older children, perhaps as part of a special project, with Indian feather headdresses. You can make drums, too, out of large juice cans. Open them on both ends and place circlets (one inch larger than the opening of the can) cut from rubber inner tube tires, at each end of the can. Punch holes one inch apart around the outside of the rubber, and lace heavy string or leather strips from each hole to the corresponding hole on the other piece of rubber. If you lace along the can tightly, the tone of the drum will be resonant.

If you use the dance in a production, or as part of a play, have the children enter in a line, with a toe-heel step, beating their drums. For the toe-heel step, put your entire weight on the forward toe for the first count, and then come down with your full weight on your heel. Continue with the next foot forward, so the step is really a walk forward or backward, however you wish to use it.

Have the children form a circle. If they are carrying drums, they should put them on the floor in front of them before they continue the dance.

For the first 4 measures, the children extend their arms upward and outward, looking at the sky as if asking for rain. Then they lower their arms and fold them in front of their chests. Repeat this 3 times (4 in all) until the end of the fourth measure. Each complete movement takes one measure.

On the fifth measure, the children stretch their arms straight out to the side and make a fist, which they use for the rest of the dance. Then they slide to the right 8 times, and reverse and slide to the left 8 times. Make sure they slide close to the floor, as if they are hugging it silently. This will bring you to the end of the eighth measure.

For the ninth measure, lift the arms (with fists) straight up in the air, taking two steps in place at the same time. In measure 10, bend down low and bring the arms (with fists) down toward the floor in 3 separate movements, taking 3 steps simultaneously in place. Hold in this position for the fourth count of the measure. Repeat these movements for measures 11 and 12.

On measures 13–16, the children do the toe-heel step, turning in place, first to the right and then to the left. If they have drums, they can pick them up and beat them during these turns. If not, have them swing their arms (still with fists), one back and one front, as they lean back and forth.

At the end, the children give one loud Indian call and repeat the dance from the beginning.

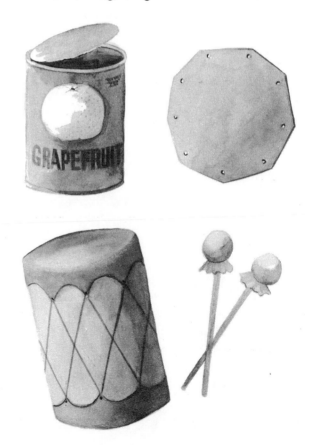

CHE CHE KOOLE (African Chant)

Each line of this very versatile chant from Ghana is sung first by the leader, and then answered by the group. Sing it loud and clear and forcefully. When the group answers, it is in exact imitation of what you sing and what you do.

In this version, start by singing the chant through once. The second time, clap as you sing, but clap 4 even beats to each measure, even though all the music is not even. The third time you sing it, clap in the rhythm of the music. After going through the chant three times, the children should know the words well enough to start moving as they sing.

Begin the dance in a circle, with you—the leader—in the center. Clap and sing the first line. The children answer, also clapping the rhythm. Repeat this pattern through the entire chant. Then silently count to yourself 4 beats, with no sound and no movement.

The second time through, stamp the rhythm with your feet as you sing. When the children answer, they stamp the rhythm, too, but this time they move toward the circle center. Use the same pattern for the next line. On the third line, turn in place as you stamp, and when the children answer, have them finish their turns facing the outside of the circle.

When the fourth answer comes, they start moving back to their places, out from the circle center. At the end of the fifth line answer, they turn and face the inside of the circle. Complete the chant again with 4 counts of silence.

The third time, move your head on each of the 4 counts of the first line. The children imitate this, in place. On the second line, move your shoulders; on the third, your arms; on the fourth, your hips, and last, your feet, stamping out the rhythm in place. Follow with the 4 counts of silence.

The fourth time through, combine the last two patterns. Have the children (on their answer) stamp their feet in rhythm as they move toward the circle center, but on the first line add the head movement, then shoulders, add arms

with the turn, hips moving back, and finally just the feet as they return to place on the last line. Finish the chant with 4 counts of silence.

Finally, do the chant in place, but let the children take over the movement completely. While they stamp the rhythm with their feet, they add any sharp body movements they want. This involves singing, counting out the rhythm, possibly turning, and moving the body all at the same time, and it is quite complex, so only attempt it with older children, starting at age eight.

VARIATION: For younger children, just sing the chant and the answer, and then clap it out. Try it walking toward the center and out again. Keep it simple and just enjoy using your voice fully and defining the rhythm with hands and feet.

Don't feel that you must restrict yourself to these patterns. Experiment with other movement possibilities and even rhythm possibilities. You might try a chorus of drummers, who beat out the rhythms as the group dances and then explores other individual rhythmic improvisations.

CHE CHE KOOLE (African Chant)

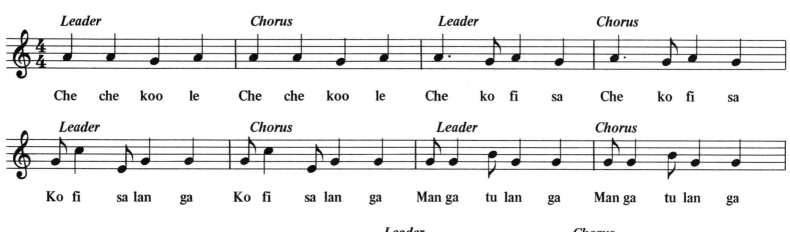

Che che koo le   Che che koo le   Che ko fi sa   Che ko fi sa

Ko fi sa lan ga   Ko fi sa lan ga   Man ga tu lan ga   Man ga tu lan ga

Aye,   A ye de   Aye,   A ye de

Che Che Koole
Che Ko Fi Sa
Ko Fi Sa Langa
Manga Tu Langa
Aye, A Ye De

pronounced:
Chay Chay Kool-ay
Chay Koe Fee Sah
Koe Fee Sah Lahnga
Mahnga Too Lahnga
Ay, Eye Yay Day

HOOP DANCING GAMES

Maybe you once saw well-dressed children rolling hoops through the park on Sundays. They used sticks to urge their wooden hoops along. Now hoops are made of plastic—light, inexpensive, and colorful—and no more sticks. Here are some new games to play with hoops.

Jumping through a Hoop

Young children love this game. You are the animal trainer, they are performing poodles. Hold the hoop upright, and call each child to run to the hoop like a dog (on four legs, not on their knees). When he gets to the hoop, have him stop and on four legs, jump through the hoop. Pat him on the head, because he did such a good trick. He wags his tail and runs back (on four legs) to his group. Call each child individually, since only one at a time has room to jump through the hoop.

The Sailboat

Two children stand inside a hoop, each with arms spread out wide, holding the hoop and leaning back against it. The children lean slowly from side to side, moving and turning like a sailboat, and then spin quickly in one direction like a top. Make sure to stop them before they get too dizzy.

The Eagle Game

This is one of the best games I know. Spread out four or five hoops on the floor in a semi-circle and explain to the children that these are not hoops but lily pads. The children are frogs, hopping in the water near the lily pads within the semi-circle, until they hear a loud sound on the piano. That is the signal that the Mean Old Wicked Eagle is flying in search of his lunch, and of course he loves to eat little frogs. When the frogs hear this sound, they must hop as quickly as they can onto a lily pad (inside a hoop) where they will be safe from the eagle. Explain that a lily pad can hold many frogs.

You are the Eagle. Play a chord on the piano, rotate your stiff wings, vibrate them and glare wickedly at the frogs as you stalk them. By the time you get to the frogs, they will all be sitting safely on lily pads. Sometimes a brave child will taunt the Eagle and want to be caught. Don't deny him and the other children this great pleasure. Just pick him up from behind, with your arms around his waist, swing him around a few times and carry him off. The class will screech with glee. Only play this game twice. Its dramatic effect is lost with too much repetition.

HOOP DANCING GAMES

The Boardwalk

Walking on a boardwalk is fun, but make sure the children know what a boardwalk is before you start, what it's made of and where it's built. Then make a boardwalk by placing hoops on the floor in a line, one touching the next. Choose a leader to head the line of children who will walk the boardwalk.

First have each child take two steps within the first hoop, and then continue without stopping right into the next hoops, taking two steps in each one. As soon as the child ahead has moved on to the next hoop, start the next child walking.

When each child has had a turn, re-form the line at the other end of the boardwalk, and start again. This time each child takes three jumps in each hoop. Count out the rhythm for them as they jump from one hoop to the next, with no time between jumps. It's not easy.

For young children, select easy things to do on the boardwalk, such as walking or galloping. Older children will enjoy doing four jumps while turning in each hoop, or skipping "crooked" by crossing the lifted leg over the other, or jumping once inside the hoop and the second time with feet apart in the outside space where the two hoops meet.

Then separate the hoops so there is space between them and leading the line yourself, run around the outside of the hoop, then between the hoops and around the other side of the next hoop—weaving in and out.

Pass the Ball

Gently

You probably know the game of "Hot Potato," in which children sit in a circle with crossed legs, or on their knees, and pass the ball from one to the other, until the music stops. The one left holding the ball is out. The circle closes in and the game starts again. It is an elimination game, and soon there is only one person left.

In my variation, the ball passes until a loud sound on the piano signals a change of direction, and on it goes. No one is "out," but each child has to listen hard and keep aware, and the result is great fun.

Play the music as it appears here for the first two ball-passes. After that, vary it, so that you stop after the second measure with a loud chord. Then stop after the fourth, then after the first, so the children do not know when the signal to reverse direction will come and must stay on guard.

BALL GAMES

Roll the Ball

Smooth and with lots of pedal

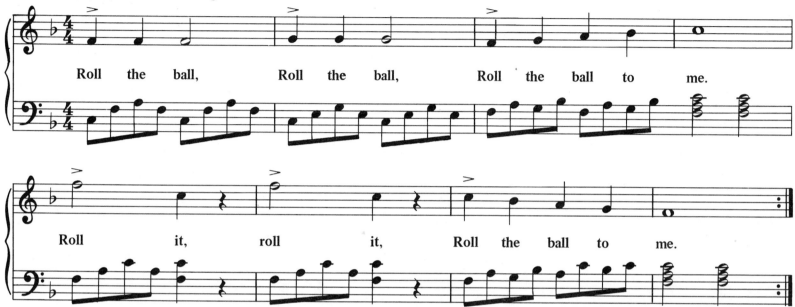

Roll the ball, Roll the ball, Roll the ball to me.

Roll it, roll it, Roll the ball to me.

This song is enormously useful for work with young children. It teaches them to listen, to release the ball at the precise moment, and to recognize musical phrasing. First have the children sing the song with you at the piano. They are to make believe they are holding a ball in their hands and roll the ball (do the actual movement) on the word "Roll." After the third roll, they have to hold on to the ball and *not* roll it, and there is a long space before the next "Roll." This is difficult and needs explaining on your part, and repetition. When the words continue and again "Roll," is mentioned, they roll the ball on that word, as before.

The next time you sing the song, substitute the word "Bounce," and then use the word "Throw." After going through the song three times, the children usually learn to hold the ball after the third movement. Emphasize this for them by putting your own hands in your lap after it and letting them imitate you.

Then have the children sit in a circle with their legs spread apart, so you can roll the ball to them. Stand in the center of the circle and sing the song. On each "Roll," roll the ball to one of the children, and on the next "Roll," he rolls it back to you. Go around the circle, giving each child a turn. You may have to remind them to hold the ball at the proper place, and not roll it back directly. When they have mastered this, let partners roll the imaginary ball to each other across the circle. And when you feel they are ready, use a real ball. Try starting with the large size and then graduate to a smaller one.

VARIATIONS: With older children you can still use this game either in a circle or with partners, but go on immediately to the words "Bounce" and "Throw" using a real ball. For extra fun (and confusion), use three balls at a time.

JUMP-ROPE JINGLES AND GAMES

These jump-rope games are difficult and should be attempted only by older children. There is a great deal to remember and count and focus on. They can be done by one child with her own rope, or by a group using the longer rope that two children turn, one at each end. Keep the rope turning at a good clip. The tunes and words are perky and peppy and really take off.

Try this jumping pattern: on the first line hop 4 times on the right foot; on the second line, hop 4 times on the left foot. On the third line hop twice on each foot; on the last line alternate feet—right-left 4 times. Actually at this point it's no longer a hop, but rather a run from one foot to the next. Repeat the entire pattern for the second stanza of each story.

Since you can jump these jingles to any pattern, try the combinations described in "Boom Boom," in the second stanza. Feel free to experiment and get the children to make up their own jumping patterns. It is a study in math, direction, focus, and ingenuity. When a child invents a unique pattern, ask her to show it and teach it to the whole group.

Young Folks, Old Folks

Spirited

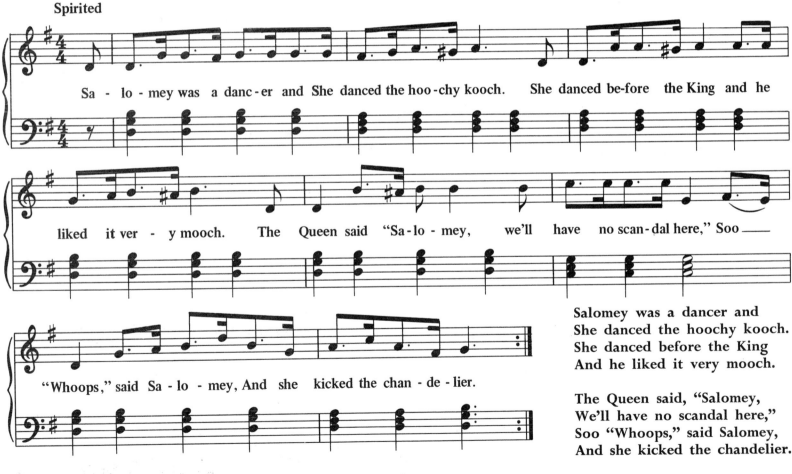

Sa-lo-mey was a danc-er and She danced the hoo-chy kooch. She danced be-fore the King and he liked it ver-y mooch. The Queen said "Sa-lo-mey, we'll have no scan-dal here," Soo— "Whoops," said Sa-lo-mey, And she kicked the chan-de-lier.

Salomey was a dancer and
She danced the hoochy kooch.
She danced before the King
And he liked it very mooch.

The Queen said, "Salomey,
We'll have no scandal here,"
Soo "Whoops," said Salomey,
And she kicked the chandelier.

JUMP-ROPE JINGLES AND GAMES

Young folks, old folks, ev-ery bod-y come, Come to the Sun-day School and have a lot of fun. Please check your chew-ing gum and rai-sins at the door, and I'll tell you Bi-ble sto-ries that you nev-er heard be-fore.

CHORUS

Young folks, old folks,
Everybody come.
Come to the meeting house
And have a lot of fun.

Please check your chewing gum
And raisins at the door,
And I'll tell you Bible stories
That you never heard before.

Sampson was a strong man,
You bet he was no fool.
He killed ten thousand Philistines
With the jawbone of a mule.

A woman named Delilah,
She cut his hair real thin,
And when he came to afterwards,
The coppers pulled him in.

CHORUS

Jonah was a sailor,
He set out for a sail.
He took a first class passage
On a transatlantic whale.

He didn't like his quarters,
Although they were the best,
So Jonah pushed the button
And the whaley did the rest.

CHORUS

The world was built in six days,
And finished on the seventh.
According to the contract,
It should have been the eleventh.

The masons they got tired,
And the carpenters wouldn't work,
So the only thing that they could do
Was fill it up with dirt.

JUMP-ROPE JINGLES AND GAMES

Boom Boom, Ain't It Great to Be Crazy?

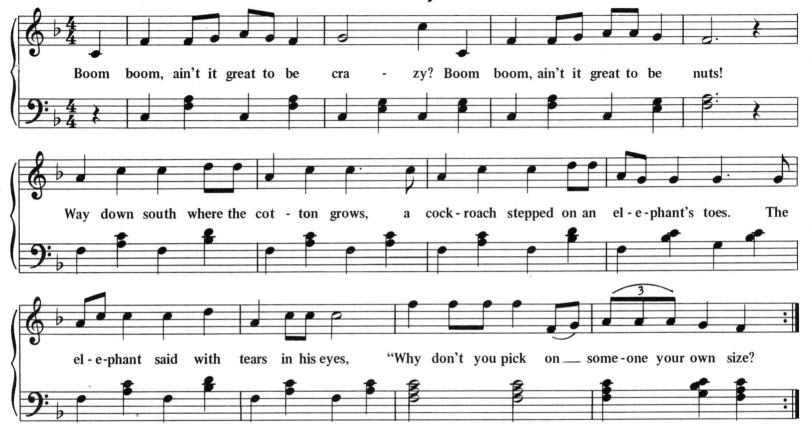

Boom boom, ain't it great to be cra - zy? Boom boom, ain't it great to be nuts!

Way down south where the cot - ton grows, a cock - roach stepped on an el - e - phant's toes. The

el - e - phant said with tears in his eyes, "Why don't you pick on ___ some - one your own size?

Way down south where the cotton grows,
A cockroach stepped on an elephant's toes.
The elephant said with tears in his eyes,
"Why don't you pick on someone your own size?"

Chorus
Boom boom, ain't it great to be cra-zy?
Boom boom, ain't it great to be nuts!

I bought a suit of combination underwear
Can't get it off, I do declare.
Wore it six months without exaggeration.
Can't get it off, cause I lost the combination.

This delightful song or chant can be jumped in many ways. Here is one possible pattern:

Choose one person to jump the first stanza, another to jump the second. The first line is a normal jump with feet together 4 times. Jump the second line with one foot in front of the other 4 times. On the third line combine the two, so the feet are together for the first and third jumps, one foot in front for the second and fourth jumps. On the last line, jump with feet together 4 times, turning as you go. If you have a small group, it's fun to have all the children jump in on the chorus; they jump 7 times and out on the 8th count leaving one child (already chosen) to jump the next stanza.